Jonathan's Journey
God's Unseen Hand

Linda Clore

"Train up a child in the way he should go: and when he is old, he will not depart from it."

Proverbs 22:6—Words from the Lord.

World rights reserved. This book or any portion thereof may not be copied or reproduced in any form or manner whatever, except as provided by law, without the written permission of the publisher, except by a reviewer who may quote brief passages in a review.

The author assumes full responsibility for the accuracy of all facts and quotations as cited in this book. The opinions expressed in this book are the author's personal views and interpretations, and do not necessarily reflect those of the publisher.

This book is provided with the understanding that the publisher is not engaged in giving spiritual, legal, medical, or other professional advice. If authoritative advice is needed, the reader should seek the counsel of a competent professional.

Copyright © 2019 Linda Clore
Copyright © 2019 ASPECT Books
ISBN-13: 978-1-4796-1011-2 (Paperback)
ISBN-13: 978-1-4796-1012-9 (ePub)
Library of Congress Control Number: 2019909451

All Bible text references are taken from the King James Version (KJV) of the Bible. Public domain.

Introduction

We claimed Proverbs 22:6. David and I prayed for a child we could raise for the Lord. God blessed us with a son. We prayed for the Lord to please name our child. As we prayed, we were impressed by the Lord to name our son, Jonathan Paul which means "Little Gift of God."

When I delivered Jonathan, I almost bled to death and had to be taken back into surgery to take care of a fibroid tumor that kept bleeding.

While in surgery, I was singing that song, "Oh That Will Be Glory For Me!" When I came out from under the anesthetic, I heard myself singing and I was embarrassed and I stopped singing.

The OB/Gyn doctor or our doctor never did charge us for that surgery! Praise the Lord! David was in colporteuring work when Jonathan was born and not making very many sales. But God took care of us. Praise the Lord! Thank you Jesus!

God spared my life so I could raise the child God gave to us for Him.

We raised Jonathan out in the country like the Lord tells us to do. (Read *Country Living* by Sister White).

In *Jonathan's Journey*, God's unseen hand has been over him and seeing him through his growing up years and out on his own and in his folly and the many times God has spared his life! God has a purpose and plan for Jonathan and for each of us.

Dedication

I dedicate this story of *Jonathan's Journey* and *God's Unseen Hand* to Jesus and to Jonathan, as God has miraculously been watching over Jonathan through his folly years and sparing his life over and over again, until He could get his attention to follow the Lord with all his heart! Praise the Lord! Thank you Jesus!

I also want to thank Jonathan's dad, David, for all the help he has been to me in raising Jonathan for the Lord and even though Jonathan went astray, the Lord has been with us all on this journey of faith to work to bring him back to follow Jesus! God gets all the praise! Keep singing the song, "I'm pressing on the upward way; New heights I'm gaining every day; Still praying as I'm onward bound; Lord, plant my feet on higher ground."

Acknowledgements

Thank you my dear and wonderful publishing company for working with me to get this story of "Jonathan's Journey" out to be an encouragement to others who have gone astray and how God watches over them and spares their life until He can get their attention to follow the Lord and do His will and not their own. And to encourage the parents to not give up hope in trusting the good Lord to spare their child in their sin and folly and to bring them back safely to the fold. Never give up! Keep praying! There's power in prayer! There's power in God's word. **Read** Proverbs 22:6; Matthew 21:22; Isaiah 49:24, 25; Jeremiah 31:3, 15-17, 33, 34; Jeremiah 29:11-14.

Dear Readers:

May this book help you see God's love for us, even when we're ignoring His still small voice. Even though we may be putting our desires above God's desires for us, God is still loving us and wooing us back to His tender loving care and helping us to see our mistakes and change our ways before it's too late.

"God's Unseen Hand!"

(Jonathan's Journey) written by Linda Clore

Written 9–30–16 to 1–19–18

"No one sees the hand that lifts the burden or beholds the light descend from the courts above. The blessing comes when by faith the soul surrenders itself to God. Then that power which no human eye can see creates a new being in the image of God." E.G. White quote from *Desire of Ages*, p. 173.

"Cast thy burden upon the LORD and He shall sustain thee: He shall never suffer the righteous to be moved." Psalm 55:22. Also read Psalm 139. One of my favorite sayings is: "It's all in God's hands. God is in control of everything!" Read *5T*, pp. 467–476.

When I think of Jonathan's life journey and all he's been through and how God's unseen hand has guided and provided and protected him over some rough and stormy roads, as he has been growing up and then out on his own and how God has been right there carrying him through it all! It makes me think of the poem: "Footprints in the Sand". God carries us through our hard times and dangerous times and follies and foolishness and sicknesses. God's unseen hand is always there when we need Him the most! In *Desire of Ages*, Sister White writes on page 348, "The Lord works continually to benefit mankind. He is ever imparting His bounties. He raises up the sick from beds of languishing. He delivers men from peril which they do not see. He commissions heavenly angels to save them from calamity

> *God carries us through our hard times and dangerous times and follies and foolishness and sicknesses. God's unseen hand is always there when we need Him the most*

to guard them from "the pestilence that walketh in darkness" and "the destruction that wasteth at noonday" (Psalm 91:6); but their hearts are unimpressed. He has given all the riches of heaven to redeem them, and yet they are unmindful of His great love... It is for our own benefit to keep every gift of God fresh in our memory. Thus faith is strengthened to claim and to receive more and more... Let us then remember the loving-kindness of the Lord, and the multitude of His tender mercies. Let the people of Israel, let us set up our stones of witness and inscribe upon them the precious story of what God has wrought for us. And as we review His dealing with us in our pilgrimage, let us, out of hearts melted with gratitude, declare, "What shall I render unto the Lord for all His benefits toward me? I will take the cup of salvation and call upon the name of the Lord. I will pay my vows unto the Lord now in the presence of all His people. Psalm 116:12-14." Also, in *Desire of Ages*, pp. 327–331, we have these words from God's prophet, Sister White, "Closer than father, mother, brother, friend, or lover is the Lord our Saviour. 'Fear not', He says, 'for I have redeemed thee. I have called thee by thy name; thou art mine.'" ... "He invites you to cast all your care upon Him; for He carries you upon His heart... In every difficulty He has His way prepared to bring relief... But many who profess to be His followers have an anxious, troubled heart, because they are afraid to trust themselves with God. They do not make a complete surrender to Him; for they shrink from the consequences that such a surrender may involve. Unless they do make this surrender, they cannot find peace. It is the love of self that brings unrest... He who walks in the way of God's commandments is walking in company with Christ and in His love the heart is at rest.... Whatever may be the evil practice, the master passion which through long indulgence binds both soul and body, Christ is able and longs to deliver. He will impart life to the soul that is 'dead in trespasses.' Ephesians 2:1. He will set free the captive that is held by weakness and misfortune and the claims of sin." Taken from *Desire of Ages* p. 203. Matthew 11:28–30, "Come unto me, all ye that labour and are heavy laden and I will give you rest. Take my yoke upon you and learn of me; for I am meek and lowly in heart: and ye shall find rest unto your souls. For my yoke is easy and my burden is light."

In *Ministry of Healing* by Sister White, she tells us on p. 71, "The heaviest burden that we bear is the burden of sin. If we were left to bear this burden, it would crush us. But the Sinless One has taken our place. 'The Lord hath laid on Him the iniquity of us all.'" Isaiah 53:6. Also, on pp. 104–107 of *Ministry of Healing*, we have this counsel, "In sympathy and compassion we are to minister to those in need of help, seeking with unselfish earnestness to lighten the woes of suffering humanity... Christ's rule of life by which every one of us must stand or fall in the judgment is, 'Whatsoever ye would that men should do to you, do ye even so to them.'" Matthew 7:12. Angels are ever present where they are most needed, with those who have the hardest battles with self to fight, and whose surroundings are the most discouraging. Weak and trembling souls who have many objectionable traits of character are their special charge... Many feel that it would be a great privilege to visit the scenes of Christ's life on earth, to walk where He trod, to look upon the lake beside which He loved to teach, and the hills and valleys on which His eyes so often rested. But we need not go to Nazareth, to Capernaum, or to Bethany, in order to walk in the steps of Jesus. We shall find His footprints beside the sick bed, in the hovels of poverty, in the crowded alleys of the great cities, and to every place where there are human hearts in need of consolation. We are to feed the hungry, clothe the naked, and comfort the suffering and afflicted. We are to minister to the despairing and to inspire hope in the hopeless... The love of Christ, manifested in unselfish ministry, will be more effective in reforming the evildoer than will the sword or the court of justice... Often the heart that hardens under reproof will melt under the love of Christ. The missionary cannot only relieve physical maladies, but he can lead the sinner to the Great Physician, who can cleanse the soul from the leprosy of sin. Through His servants, God designs that the sick, the unfortunate, and those possessed of evil spirits shall hear His voice. Through His human agencies He desires to be a comforter such as the world knows not... Christ walks unseen through our streets. With messages of mercy, He comes to our homes. With all who are seeking to minister in His name, He waits to co-operate. He is in the midst of us, to heal and to bless, if we will receive Him."

In *Ministry of Healing* pp. 228–230, we read, "To those who desire prayer for their restoration to health, it should be made plain that the violation of God's law, either natural or spiritual, is sin, and that in order for them to receive His blessing, sin must be confessed and forsaken..." "If we confess our sins, he is faithful and just to forgive our sins and to cleanse us from all unrighteousness." 1 John 1:9 Also, in 1 John 2:1 it says, "My little children, these things write I unto you, that ye sin not. And if any man sin, we have an advocate with the Father, Jesus Christ the righteous." Continuing in *Ministry of Healing* on pp. 229 and 230, Sister White writes, "He knows each individual by name and cares for each as if there were not another upon the earth for whom He gave His beloved Son. Because God's love is so great and so unfailing, the sick should be encouraged to trust in Him and be cheerful. To be anxious about themselves tends to cause weakness and disease. If they will rise above depression and gloom, their prospect of recovery will be better; for 'the eye of the Lord is upon them' that hope in His mercy." Psalm 33:18. In prayer for the sick, it should be remembered that, 'we know not what we should pray for as we ought.' Romans 8:26. We do not know whether the blessing we desire will be best or not. Therefore, our prayers should include this thought: 'Lord, thou knowest every secret of the soul. Thou art acquainted with these persons. Jesus, their Advocate, gave His life for them. His love for them is greater than ours can possibly be. If, therefore, it is for Thy glory and the good of the afflicted ones, we ask, in the name of Jesus, that they may be restored to health. If it be not Thy will that they may be restored, we ask that Thy grace may comfort and Thy presence sustain them in their sufferings. God knows the end from the beginning. He is acquainted with the hearts of all men. He reads every secret of the soul. He knows whether those for whom prayer is offered would or would not be able to endure the trials that would come upon them should they live. He knows whether their lives would be a blessing or a curse to themselves and to the world. This is one reason why, while presenting our petitions with earnestness, we should say, 'Nevertheless not my will, but Thine be done'. Luke 22:42." Sister White continues to write on p. 230, "The consistent course is to commit our desires to our all-wise heavenly Father, and then, in perfect confidence, trust all to Him. We know that God hears us if we ask according to His will. There are cases where God works decidedly by His divine power in the restoration of health. But not all the sick are healed. Many are laid away to sleep in Jesus. John on the Isle of Patmos was bidden to write: 'Blessed are the dead which die in the Lord from henceforth: Yea, saith the Spirit, that they may rest from their labors; and their works do follow them.' Revelation 14:13. From this we see that if persons are not raised to health, they should not, on this account be judged as wanting in faith."

Sister White continues on p. 231 to share this information, "We all desire immediate and direct answers to our prayers and are tempted to become discouraged when the answer is delayed or comes in an unlooked for form. But God is too wise and good to answer our prayers always at just the time and in just the manner we desire… Our desires and interests should be lost in His will. These experiences that test faith are for our benefit… Believing that they will be healed in answer to prayer, some fear to do anything that might seem to indicate a lack of faith. But they should not neglect to set their affairs in order as they would desire to do if they expected to be removed by death. Nor should they fear to utter words of encouragement or counsel which at the parting hour they wish to speak to their loved ones. Those who seek healing by prayer should not neglect to make use of the remedial agencies within their reach." On p. 233 Sister White makes this statement: "While He did not give countenance to drug medication, He sanctioned the use of the simple and natural remedies. When we have prayed for the recovery of the sick, whatever the outcome of the case, let us not lose faith in God. If we are called upon to meet bereavement, let us accept the bitter cup, remembering that a Father's hand holds it to our lips. But should health be restored, it should not be forgotten that the recipient of healing mercy is placed under renewed obligation to the Creator."

Sister White on p. 480 tells us this, "Many who profess to be Christ's followers have an anxious, troubled heart because they are afraid to trust themselves with God. They do not make a complete surrender to Him, for they shrink from the consequences that such a surrender may involve. Unless they do make this surrender, they cannot find peace... Worry is blind and cannot discern the future; but Jesus sees the end from the beginning. In every difficulty, He has His way prepared to bring relief. 'No good thing will He withhold from them that walk uprightly.' Psalm 84:11." God's unseen hand is always there to guide and direct and provide and protect and heal and answer prayers. We need to show faith in God's power to help us in any circumstance and remember that God's unseen hand is always there to hold us up and see us through our every difficulty. On p. 511 *Ministry of Healing* Sister White gives us this advice, "All are pressed with urgent cares, burdens and duties, but the more difficult your position and the heavier your burdens, the more you need Jesus." On p. 489 she says this, "All our sufferings and sorrows, all our temptations and trials, all our sadness and griefs, all our persecutions and privations, in short, all things work together for our good. All experiences and circumstances are God's workmen whereby good is brought to us. It reminds me of the many times God's unseen hand has watched over our son, Jonathan through his life and has spared his life so very many times!

Like the time when he was two and a half years old, he was playing outside and I was burning the trash, and I told Jonathan not to go near the fire. I got busy doing something else, and Jonathan was curious about that smoke coming up out of the trash can and so he peeked over the trash can to get a better look and his hat caught on fire! The Lord let me see what happened and I dashed over to him and ripped the flaming hat off his head! Neither of us were hurt! Thanks to God's unseen hand watching over us! Praise the Lord!

One time dad set Jonathan in back of our pickup truck in the yard, and he went to move the truck, and Jonathan fell out and was right where the truck tire was ready to roll over him, but God's unseen hand let a bucket from the back of the truck roll out and fall under the tire and it stopped dad from rolling the truck over our little boy! Thank you Jesus! Another time, as a child growing up, he climbed up in a tree 25 feet up and fell out! He landed just a few inches from two iron spikes sticking up out of the ground, that could have gone right through him! Again God spared his life by God's unseen hand! Thank you Jesus! One time, as a little boy, he drank Clorox®, thinking it was water in the jug and God's unseen hand saved him from that experience! Praise God!

Sister White says in *1 Selected Messages* p. 190, "We should now consider that our life is swiftly passing away, that we are not safe one moment unless our life is hid with Christ in God."

As Jonathan grew up and went to our church schools and academy and college, he let himself get in with the wrong crowd and began bad habits of drinking and smoking and drugging. Satan was out to destroy his life, but God's unseen hand was always there watching over him in his folly. John 10:10 says, "The thief cometh not but for to steal, and to kill and to destroy: I am come that they might have life, and that they might have it more abundantly."

We dedicated Jonathan to the Lord before he was even born and when he was born, we had him dedicated to the Lord at church. He was baptized at eight years old. By the time he was three years old, he had memorized over 500 KJV Bible verses and where they were found. At three years old he said, "I want to be a preacher." We knew God had plans for Jonathan, but we also knew Satan had his plans to stop God's plans for our son! We claimed Proverbs 22:6, as we raised Jonathan for the Lord, "Train up a child in the way he should go: and when he is old, he will not depart from it."

But as he got out on his own, he went farther and farther from what he knew was right. Like the old saying goes, "You can lead a horse to water, but you can't make him drink." We had led Jonathan as a child in the way he should go, but there comes a time in everyone's life, when they have to choose for themselves, which road they're going to walk on. Jonathan made the choice to walk on the broad and popular road that ends in destruction. Matthew 7:13, 14 says, "Enter ye in at the strait gate: for wide is the gate and broad is the way that leadeth to destruction, and many there be which go in thereat. Because strait is the gate, and narrow is the way, which leadeth to life, and few there be that find it."

In the *Ministry of Healing* book by E.G. White, we read these encouraging words on pp. 89–94, "Jesus knows the circumstances of every soul. The greater the sinner's guilt, the more he needs a Saviour. His heart of divine love and sympathy is drawn out most of all for the one who is most hopelessly entangled in the snares of the enemy. With His own blood He has signed the emancipation papers of the race. Jesus does not desire those who have been purchased at such a cost to become the sport of the enemy's temptations. He does not desire us to be overcome and perish... In the synagogue at Capernaum, Jesus was speaking of His mission to set free the slaves of sin. He was interrupted by a shriek of terror... Jesus rebuked the demon, saying, 'Hold thy peace, and come out of him. And when the devil had thrown him in the midst, he came out of him, and hurt him not.' Luke 4:35. The cause of this man's affliction also was in his own life. He had been fascinated with the pleasures of sin and had thought to make life a grand carnival. Intemperance and frivolity perverted the noble attributes of his nature, and Satan took entire control of him. Remorse came too late. When he would have sacrificed wealth and pleasure to gain his lost manhood he had become helpless in the grasp of the evil one... The demoniac partially comprehended that he was in the presence of One who could set him free; but when he tried to come within reach of that mighty hand, another's will held him, another's words found utterance through him. The conflict between the power of Satan and his own desire for freedom was terrible. It seemed that the tortured man must lose his life in the struggle with the foe that had been the ruin of his manhood. But the Saviour spoke with authority and set the captive free. The man who had been possessed stood before the wondering people in the freedom of self-possession. With glad voice he praised God for deliverance... There are multitudes today as truly under the power of the evil spirits as was the demoniac of Capernaum. All who willfully depart from God's commandments are placing themselves under the control of Satan. Many a man tampers with evil, thinking that he can break away at pleasure; but he is lured on and on, until he finds himself controlled by a will stronger than his own. He cannot escape its mysterious power. Secret sin or master passion may hold him a captive as helpless as was the demoniac of Capernaum. Yet his condition is not hopeless. God does not control our minds without our consent; but every man is free to choose what power he will have to rule over him. None have fallen so low, none are so vile, but that they may find deliverance in Christ. The demoniac, in place of prayer, could utter only the words of Satan; yet the heart's unspoken appeal was heard. No cry from a soul in need, though it fail of utterance in words, will be unheeded. Those who consent to enter into covenant with God are not left to the power of Satan or to the infirmity of their own nature. 'Shall the prey be taken from the mighty, or the lawful captive delivered?... Thus saith the Lord, Even the captives of the mighty shall be taken away, and the prey of the terrible shall be delivered: for I will contend with him that contendeth with thee, and I will save thy children'. Isaiah 49:24, 25. Marvelous will be the transformation wrought in him who by faith opens the door of the heart to the Saviour. 'Say unto them, As I live, saith the Lord God, I have no pleasure in the death of the wicked; but that the wicked turn from his way and live.' Ezekiel 33:11. 'And if it seem evil unto you to serve the Lord, choose you this day whom ye will serve:... but as for me and my house, we will serve the Lord.' Joshua 24:15. Henceforth, Christ's followers are to look upon Satan as a conquered foe. Upon the cross, Jesus was to gain the victory for them; that victory He desired them to accept as their own... The omnipotent power of the Holy Spirit is the defense of every contrite soul. No one who in penitence and faith has claimed His protection will Christ permit to pass under the enemy's power... the rainbow of promise encircling the throne on high is an everlasting testimony that 'God so loved the world that He gave His only begotten Son that whosoever believeth in Him should not perish, but have everlasting life'. John 3:16. It testifies to the universe that God will never forsake His children in the struggle with evil. It is an assurance to us of strength and protection as long as the throne itself shall endure."

> *He was out on the highway, drunk riding his bike in the rain, and he wrecked his bike and fell onto the side of the highway*

There was a time, while out on his own, drugging and drinking, Jonathan rode his bike 15 miles in the dark to get some alcohol and on the way home, after drinking his alcohol, he was out on the highway, drunk riding his bike in the rain, and he wrecked his bike and fell onto the side of the highway. There was a piece of grass stuck on his glasses and in his drunkenness he thought maybe his retina in his eye had been torn, and he was afraid and went staggering up to a house to get help in his drunken condition. The people called the police. The police came and took him and his bike back to his apartment. He was okay and not hurt! God's unseen hand saw him through another accident. Praise the Lord! The devil tried again to take his life in a terrible car accident when he was with some druggie friends who were drugging and drinking and driving fast down the highway and just before the car went out of control and rolled over and smashed into a tree, the Lord impressed Jonathan, sitting in the back seat, to lie down in the seat. As he obeyed and laid down in the seat, the top of the car smashed in, as it rolled over and hit into the tree. Jonathan's life was spared again with no injuries! God's unseen hand was there again to save him from danger and death! Praise the Lord!

Then there was the time the devil tried to take his life again! Jonathan is legally blind and can't see to drive a car and has no driver's license. But with the strong desire for more alcohol, he took his grandma's car keys and at night drove her car around 15 miles in the rain late at night through construction work out on the highway to get him some more alcohol to drink! The Lord got him and the car safely through all the construction, as he sped along drunk and on marijuana! When he got out of the car to purchase his alcohol, the car door slammed shut in the wind and rain and locked him out of the car. There was a pay phone beside the car where he had parked and he called home, collect and told us where he was and what he had done and for us to please come and get him. I drove grandma's car back to her, and David drove Jonathan back to his apartment. What a scare that was to find out what he had done! We were so very thankful he was okay! Again, God's unseen hand was over Jonathan, sparing his life for the plan God has for him! Thank you Jesus!

We always keep praying for our son that God will protect him in his folly and spare his life and convert him! (For those who don't know what pay phones are—they used to have telephones in phone booths stationed around in different places where people could drop their money in the phone and make telephone calls that way, or if they had no money, they could call the operator on the phone and call collect to the person they wanted to talk to. Cell phones have taken the place of pay phones).

There was a time when God's unseen hand was seen when Jonathan was in the big city with his drinking and drugging friends, and they had partied big time at night, and Jonathan went to sleep in his drugged and drunken condition and laid down in a driveway entrance of a company where trucks back in and unload their merchandise. There he was asleep in his drugged and drunken stupor, and the devil thought, "Now I have him where I want him!" In the early morning hour, a big van truck backed in to unload his load and didn't see Jonathan laying on the pavement asleep and the truck ran right over his chest! He was taken to the hospital, and we were notified and we hurried to the hospital. They had found, on examination, that he had no serious injuries! They checked him over for internal bleeding and any broken bones, and they couldn't find anything wrong with him! They dismissed him to go home with us. On the front of his shirt were the tire marks where the truck had rolled right over his chest! God's unseen hand had again watched over our son, Jonathan! The devil's plan to take his life in his folly was again stopped! Thank you Jesus! Jonathan has kept his guardian angel working overtime! Time and time again God has intervened to save Jonathan's life! Praise the Lord! God keeps giving him more time to repent and come back to following the Lord. Thank you Lord!

Jonathan has been in fights while drinking and drugging with his friends and injured badly and left injured and bloody and beside one of his eyes was a big gash, and he needed to be taken to the Emergency room for stitches. He had a swollen black eye for some time, but no head injuries or broken bones! Again Jonathan had God's unseen hand watching over him! Praise the Lord! Thank you Jesus!

He has been suicidal on his drugs and alcohol and one time, while out on his own, he took an overdose of his drugs and then got scared and called me on the phone and told me what he had done! I hurried and drove my car to his apartment and gave him activated charcoal with a lot of water and rushed him to the Emergency room and they gave him more activated charcoal and flew him by helicopter to the big medical center in Kansas City to get him checked over and he recovered with no damage from his overdose! There again was seen God's unseen hand at work fighting back the devil, trying to destroy Jonathan! Praise the Lord! God saved Jonathan again and spared his life! We keep praying for Jonathan's safety while living in sinful pleasure. We keep claiming Proverbs 22:6, "Train up a child in the way he should go, and when he is old, he will not depart from it."

Jonathan, when he was around 27 years old, was living out on his own smoking and drugging and drinking and abusing his doctor's medicines and taking more valium medicine than he should and not living a healthy lifestyle. One day he felt paralysis in his feet and began to stumble around and fall and not able to walk right. We took him to the hospital and they tested him and found he was going paralyzed in all his extremities! They admitted him to the hospital to find the cause of what was happening. The paralysis began to go into his internal organs and then in his lungs and throat and he couldn't get his breath! They were just ready to do a tracheotomy! We prayed and asked God to please spare his life. The paralysis began to remove from his internal organs and in time all the paralysis was healed, except in his ankles. They remained paralyzed. He had to become a wheelchair patient. But God had spared his life and gave him more time to come back to the Lord and be saved! Praise the Lord! Thank you Jesus! Again God's unseen hand was revealed in this terrifying and horrible experience! But this experience of God's miraculous healing didn't change Jonathan and convert him. He just remained in his old lifestyle of sinful pleasures and now began a life of sin, living in a wheelchair. God is longsuffering and merciful and kind and patiently dealt with Jonathan in his folly. 2 Peter 3:9, "The Lord is not slack concerning his promise, as some men count slackness; but is longsuffering to us-word, not willing that any should perish, but that all should come to repentance".

For six and a half years I cared for Jonathan in our home while his paralysis worked out of his body! All this time I tried to win him back to the Lord, but as soon as he was well enough to function on his own, he got his own apartment and began his smoking again, along with his drinking and drugging, etc. One day when he was drunk and drugged up, he purchased a hunter's knife and had it laying beside his chair and was tempted to take his life and end his misery! But again God's unseen hand intervened, and Jonathan gave the knife to us so he wouldn't take his life! Thank you dear Jesus for keeping Satan under control and sparing Jonathan's life! Praise the Lord!

There was a time when Jonathan was recuperating from his paralysis, while I cared for him in our home that he decided he'd rather be cared for in a nursing home, since he could now sit up in the wheelchair okay. The old desires to return to his old life of sinful pleasures were growing stronger and the urges to smoke, etc. were calling him to go where he could do as he pleased. So, he was admitted to the nursing home and he was back to a lot of doctor's drugs and a bad diet and dairy products and junk foods and smoking and coffee and tea and meat, etc. He came down with diabetes and eventually, the head nurse told me Jonathan had gangrene in both legs and she was going to have to schedule him to have both his legs cut off! I said, "No! I'll bring him back home and care for him and with the Lord's help, save both his legs!" So, I brought him home and did natural remedies on his legs and gave him good healthy vegetarian meals with no meat and no smoking and no pop, junk foods and no tea and coffee and no dairy or sweets and with lots of prayer and hard work, God's unseen hand had touched and healed him and saved his two legs from being cut off! He still has a small scar on his right leg from the activated charcoal poultices I used to heal him with, along with a lot of other natural remedies. Praise God for natural remedies and the power of prayer! Thank you Jesus! Praise God from whom all blessings flow!

Then, another time he chose to be cared for in the nursing home and this time on his flunky lifestyle in the nursing home, he developed a terribly bad bed sore! They had to do surgery on his bedsore to try and heal it! But nothing they did would get it well! We dismissed him and brought him home and with God's unseen hand touching him and healing him through the natural remedies and hard work and lots of prayer and good healthy vegetarian food and no meat and off his smoking and junk foods and tea and coffee and dairy and pop and sweets, he was well again! Thank you Jesus! Praise the Lord! Jonathan was seeing the contrast in his flunky lifestyle versus God's way of living, but this didn't stop him from choosing to go back again into his life of sinful pleasures in a nursing home again and eventually was on 32 doctor's drugs and smoking and picking up street drugs from friends and back to a meat diet and tea and coffee and pop and junk foods and lots of doctor's drugs and dairy products and lots of sweets, etc. His bedsore returned and he felt himself growing weaker and weaker and he felt like he was dying, he said. He asked to come home and get well! Again, he returned home and with God's unseen hand upon him, he returned to good health and on only five medicines and back to God's way of living, except this time he chewed tobacco, but didn't smoke. His bedsore healed up again from good care and using God's natural remedies and lots of prayer and a good healthy vegetarian diet and no sweets or pop and no junk foods, no tea or coffee and no dairy products or meats. Then he went to taking diet pills, saying he wanted to hurry and lose all this weight he'd gained in the nursing home and still had his diabetes.

He remained two and a half years home with us, when we saw what his diet pills were doing to him. We said, no more of those will be allowed and we said we'll cut you down on your chewing tobacco and help you off nicotine. He became upset and became depressed that he couldn't have his lifestyle the way he wanted living at home, so he chose to go back to a nursing home where he could live the way he wanted to live and not be told what to do. In those two and a half years he was home with us, we tried to help him come back to the Lord this time with all his heart and cut loose from his sinful pleasures for Jesus, but he was determined he wanted to return to a nursing home. He was admitted to the hospital because of his depression. Then he wanted them to find him a nursing home from the hospital and not return back home. We claimed James 1:5 for wisdom and knowledge to know what the Lord would have us to do and to help Jonathan make the right decision what he wanted in life and that he'd choose Jesus with all his heart and not want to return back to his old bad habits like Proverbs 26:11 says, "As a dog returneth to his vomit, so a fool returneth to his folly". And Proverbs 5:21, 22 "For the ways of man are before the eyes of the Lord and he pondereth all his goings. His own iniquities shall take the wicked himself, and he shall be holden with the cords of his sins." Read Romans 6. God's unseen hand has been upon Jonathan through his life of sin and folly. We continue to pray for his conversion and claim promises like: James 4:7, 8; Mark 10:27; Luke 1:37; and Luke 4:40, "Now when the sun was setting, all they that had any sick with diverse diseases brought them unto him; and he laid his hands on every one of them, and healed them."

We pray God's unseen hand will again be placed on Jonathan and heal his depression and free him of Satan's hold on him, and that he'll choose to surrender all to Jesus and be an overcomer in the power and strength God can give him like 1 Corinthians 15:57, 58 promises: "But thanks be to God, which giveth us the victory through our Lord Jesus Christ. Therefore, my beloved brethren, be ye steadfast, unmovable, always abounding in the work of the Lord, forasmuch as ye know that your labour is not in vain in the Lord." Also, we claim Philippians 4:13, "I can do all things through Christ, which strengtheneth me." Also Isaiah 49:25; Matthew 21:22; Philippians 4:6, 7; Acts 11:21, "And the hand of the Lord was with them: and a great number believed, and turned unto the Lord." We continue to claim Proverbs 22;6, "Train up a child in the way he should go: and when he is old, he will not depart from it." Jonathan is now 46 years old. Time is running out! Sister White, in her book *Last Day Events* writes on p. 42, "The end is near. This is that which Jesus would have us keep ever before us – the shortness of time." She also says on p. 211, "Many who have strayed from the fold will come back to follow the great Shepherd... God has in reserve a firmament of chosen ones that will yet shine forth amidst the darkness, revealing clearly to an apostate world the transforming power of obedience to His law." Again she writes on p. 222, "Satan is now using every device in this sealing time to keep the minds of God's people from present truth and to cause them to waver." Continue reading on p. 156, "But how often have

> *We pray God's unseen hand will again be placed on Jonathan and heal his depression and free him of Satan's hold on him, and that he'll choose to surrender all to Jesus and be an overcomer in the power and strength God can give him*

the professed advocates of the truth proved the greatest obstacle to its advancement! The unbelief indulged, the doubts expressed, the darkness cherished, encourage the presence of evil angels, and open the way for the accomplishment of Satan's devices."

In *Desire of Ages* by E.G. White, she tells us on pp. 37 and 38, "Satan was exulting that he had succeeded in debasing the image of God in humanity. Then Jesus came to restore in man the image of his Maker. None but Christ can fashion anew the character that has been ruined by sin. He came to expel the demons that had controlled the will. He came to lift us up from the dust, to reshape the marred character after the pattern of His divine character, and to make it beautiful with His own glory." Also, on pp. 673 and 674, Sister White says, "Christ's solemn warning was a call to heart searching. Peter needed to distrust himself and to have a deeper faith in Christ... When on the Sea of Galilee he was about to sink, he cried, '"LORD save me.' Matthew 14:30. Then the hand of Christ was outstretched to grasp his hand. So now if he had cried to Jesus, Save me from myself, he would have been kept." In the book "My Life Today" by Sister White, she gives this advice, "Often our trials are such that they seem almost unbearable, and without help from God, they are indeed unbearable. Unless we rely upon Him we shall sink under the burden of responsibilities that bring only sadness and grief. But if we make Christ our dependence, we shall not sink under trial. When all seems dark and unexplainable, we are to trust in His love; we must repeat the words that Christ has spoken to our souls, 'What I do thou knowest not now, but thou shalt know hereafter'... What shall have the power of the Highest with us... Jesus stands by our side... As the trials come, the power of God will come with them." Sister White goes on to say on p. 322, "Behold I come quickly: hold that fast which thou hast, that no man take thy crown. Revelation 3:11". (Don't let Satan steal your crown either! John 10:10, 'The thief cometh not, but for to steal, and to kill and to destroy: I am come that they might have life, and that they might have it more abundantly.') Sister White continues to say, "Decisions may be made in a moment that fix one's condition forever... But remember, it would take the work of a lifetime to recover what a moment of yielding to temptation and thoughtlessness throws away... By a momentary act of will, you may place yourself in the power of Satan, but it will require more than a momentary act of will to break his fetters and reach for a higher, holier life. The purpose may be formed, the work begun, but its accomplishment will require toil, time and perseverance, patience and sacrifice. The man who deliberately wanders from God in the full blaze of light will find, when he wishes to set his face to return, that briars and thorns have grown up in his path, and he must not be surprised or discouraged if he is compelled to travel long with torn and bleeding feet. The most fearful and most to be dreaded evidence of man's fall from a better state is the fact that it costs so much to get back. The way of return can be gained only by hard fighting, inch by inch, every hour... Those who win heaven will put forth their noblest efforts and will labor with all long-suffering, that they may reap the fruit of toil. There is a hand that will open wide the gates of Paradise to those who have stood the test of temptation and kept a good conscience by giving up the world, its honors its applause, for the love of Christ, thus confessing Him before men and waiting with all patience for Him to confess them before His Father and the holy angels. Keep the conscience tender, that you may hear the faintest whisper of the voice that spake as never a man spoke."

Sister White gives this counsel in her book *Desire of Ages* on p. 301, "Through affliction God reveals to us the plague spots in our characters, that by His grace we may overcome our faults. Unknown chapters in regard to ourselves are opened to us, and the test comes, whether we will accept the reproof and the counsel of God. When brought into trial, we are not to fret and complain. We should not rebel, or worry ourselves out of the hand of Christ. We are to humble the soul before God... God's word for the sorrowing is, 'I have seen his ways, and will heal him'... The highest evidence of nobility in a Christian is self-control." Over on p. 300, Sister White has these words to share, "The proud heart strives to earn salvation; but both our title to heaven and our fitness for it are found in the righteousness of Christ. The Lord can do nothing toward the recovery of man until, convinced of his own weakness and stripped of all self-sufficiency, he yields himself to the control of God. Then he can receive the gift that God is waiting to bestow. From the soul that feels his need, nothing is withheld. He has unrestricted access to Him in whom all fullness dwells." Continue to read on pp. 634 to 636 the words of God's prophet, Sister White, "After He had given the signs of His coming, Christ said, 'When ye see these things come to pass, know ye that the kingdom of God is nigh at hand.' 'Take ye heed, watch and pray.' God has always given men warning of coming judgments... The word came to Noah, 'Come thou and all thy house into the ark; for thee have I seen righteous before me.' Noah obeyed and was saved. The message came to Lot, 'Up, get you out of this place; for the Lord will destroy this city.' Genesis 7:1; 19:14. Lot placed himself under the guardianship of the heavenly messengers and was saved. So Christ's disciples were given warning of the destruction of Jerusalem. Those who watched for the sign of the coming ruin, and fled from the city, escaped the destruction. So now we are given warning of Christ's second coming and of the destruction to fall upon the world. Those who heed the warning will be saved… As Enoch, Noah, Abraham and Moses each declared the truth for his time, so will Christ's servants now give the special warning for their generation… Earthly passions, corrupt thoughts, take possession of the mind. The evil servant eats and drinks with the drunken, unites with the world in pleasure seeking… He mingles with the world. Like grows with like in transgression. It is a fearful assimilation. With the world he is taken in the snare… 'If therefore thou shalt not watch, I will come on thee as a thief, and thou shalt not know what hour I will come upon thee.' Revelation 3:3. The advent of Christ will surprise the false teachers. They are saying, 'Peace and safety'. 'Sudden destruction cometh upon them.' 1 Thessalonians 5:3. …The world full of rioting, full of godless pleasure, is asleep, asleep in carnal security. Men are putting afar off the coming of the Lord… We will go deeper into pleasure loving… Everything in the world is in agitation. The signs of the times are ominous. Coming events cast their shadows before. The Spirit of God is withdrawing from the earth, and calamity follows calamity by sea and by land. There are tempests, earthquakes, fires, floods, murders of every grade. Who can read the future? Where is security? There is assurance in nothing that is human or earthly. Rapidly are men ranging themselves under the banner they have chosen. Restlessly are they waiting and watching the movement of their leaders. There are those who are waiting and watching and working for our Lord's appearing. Another class are falling into line under the generalship of the first great apostate. Few believe with heart and soul that we have a hell to shun and a heaven to win. The crisis is stealing gradually upon us. The sun shines in the heavens, passing over its usual round and the heavens still declare the glory of God. Men are still eating and drinking, planting and building, marrying and giving in marriage. Merchants are still buying and selling. Men are jostling one against another, contending for the highest place. Pleasure lovers are still crowding to theaters, horse races, gambling hells. The highest excitement prevails, yet probation's hour is fast closing and every case is about to be eternally decided. Satan sees that his time is short. He has set all his agencies at work that men may be deceived, deluded, occupied and entranced, until the day of probation shall be ended and the door of mercy be forever shut. Solemnly there come to us down through the centuries the warning words of our Lord from the Mount of Olives: 'Take heed to yourselves, lest at any time your hearts be overcharged with surfeiting, and drunkenness, and cares of this life, and so that day come upon you unawares. Watch ye therefore, and pray always, that ye may be accounted worthy to escape all these things that shall come to pass, and to stand before the Son of men.'"

God's door of mercy is shut at the close of probation. This is a serious and solemn time we should be preparing for right now and examining ourselves and getting rid of our sins, so we can stand without a mediator during the 7 last plagues, during the great time of trouble. It makes me think of the Pope's door of mercy he said will shut on November 20, 2016 and it will be severity for those who don't go along with him! We know this can mean possibly the Sunday Laws passed and persecution and fines and imprisonment and inducement and no buy and no sell can begin for God's people who will remain true and loyal to God's 7th day Bible Sabbath Genesis 2:1–3, and all God's 10 Commandments Exodus 20:1–17, and not go along with the Sunday Laws passed forcing people to keep the man-made Sunday sabbath. Read *Last Day Events* by E.G. White pp. 255–256 and *Great Controversy* chapters 38 and 39. There's a great battle going on between Christ and Satan over whose side we'll choose to be on, Christ's or Satan's, God's 7th day Sabbath or Satan's Sunday sabbath? We all are going to have to make this serious decision! This will be the test we all will have to take and live with the consequences of our choice we make!

Sister White says on p. 659 in *Desire of Ages* book, "They are to open the soul to the bright beams of the Sun of Righteousness. With hearts cleansed by Christ's most precious blood, in full consciousness of His presence, although unseen, they are to hear His words, 'Peace I leave with you, My peace I give unto you: not as the world giveth, give I unto you.' John 14:27. Our Lord says, Under conviction of sin, remember that I died for you. When oppressed and persecuted and afflicted for My sake and the gospel's, remember My love, so great that for you I gave My life. When your duties appear stern and severe, and your burdens too heavy to bear, remember that for your sake, I endured the cross, despising the shame. When your heart shrinks from the trying ordeal, remember that your Redeemer liveth to make intercession for you."

In the book *Patriarchs and Prophets* by Sister White, we read on p. 279 her advice, "By obedience the people were to give evidence of their faith. So all who hope to be saved by the merits of the blood of Jesus Christ should realize that they themselves have something to do in securing their salvation. While it is Christ only that can redeem us from the penalty of transgression, we are to turn from sin to obedience. Man is to be saved by faith, not by works; yet his faith must be shown by his works. God has given His Son to die as a propitiation for sin, He has manifested the light of truth, the way of life; He has given facilities, ordinances and privileges, and now man must co-operate with these saving agencies; he must appreciate and use the helps that God has provided—believe and obey all the divine requirements."

In *5T* by E.G. White pp. 345 and 346 this is written: "Character will be tested. Christ will be revealed in us if we are indeed branches of the living vine. We shall be patient, kind and forbearing, cheerful amid frets and irritations. Day by day and year by year we shall conquer self and grow into a noble heroism. This is our allotted task; but it cannot be accomplished without continual help from Jesus, resolute decision, unwavering purpose, continual watchfulness and unceasing prayer. Each one has a personal battle to fight. Each must win his own way through struggles and discouragements. Those who decline the struggle lose the strength and joy of victory. No one, not even God, can carry us to heaven, unless we make the necessary effort on our part. We must put features of beauty into our lives. We must expel the unlovely natural traits that make us unlike Jesus. While God works in us to will and to do of His own good pleasure, we must work in harmony with Him. The religion of Christ transforms the heart. It makes the worldly-minded man heavenly-minded... He forms correct habits, for the gospel of Christ has become to him a savor of life unto life. Now while probation lingers, it does not become one to pronounce sentence upon others and look to himself as a model man. Christ is our model; imitate Him, plant your feet in His steps... We are not to condemn others; this is not our work; but we should love one another and pray for one another. When we see one err from the truth, then we may weep over him as Christ wept over Jerusalem... 'If any of you do err from the truth, and one convert him; let him know, that he which converteth the sinner from the error of his way shall save a soul from death, and shall hide a multitude of sins.' What a great missionary work is this! How much more Christ-like than for poor, fallible mortals to be ever accusing and condemning those who do not exactly meet their minds. Let us remember that Jesus knows us individually and is touched with the feeling of our infirmities. He knows the wants of each of His creatures and reads the hidden, unspoken grief of every heart... He cares for His feeble, sickly, wandering sheep. He knows them all by name. The distress of every sheep and every lamb of His flock touches His heart of sympathizing love, and the cry for aid reaches His ear... 'My sheep wandered through all the mountains, and upon every high hill: yea, My flock was scattered upon all the face of the earth, and none did search or seek after them.' Jesus cares for each one as though there were not another individual on the face of the earth."

This makes me think of the song, "The Ninety and Nine". (Read Ezekiel 3 and Ezekiel 33). Still in 5T pp. 546 and 547 we read, "Movements are being set on foot to enslave the consciences of those who would be loyal to God. The lawmaking powers will be against God's people. Every soul will be tested. Oh, that we would, as a people, be wise for ourselves, and by precept and example impart that wisdom to our children! Every position of our faith will be searched into; and if we are not thorough Bible students, established, strengthened, and settled, the wisdom of the world's great men will lead us astray... Every soul who truly believes the truth will have corresponding works. All will be earnest and solemn, and unwearied in their efforts to win souls to Christ. If the truth is first planted deep in their own souls, then they will seek to plant it in the hearts of others... The Word of God should be studied and obeyed, then the heart will find rest and peace and joy, and the aspirations will tend heavenward; but when truth is kept apart from the life, in the outer court, the heart is not warmed with the glowing fire of God's goodness... The Bible, God's pure, holy Word, must be his counselor and guide, the controlling power of his life. It gives forth its lessons to us if we will take them to heart."

While I had Jonathan home with me those two and a half years, God gave me several dreams, telling me to study the Bible with Jonathan. So, I'd read the Bible to him and we'd discuss the Bible together and study Bible study lessons together on what we believe from the Bible. We'd watch DVDs we purchased for him to learn our beliefs from the Bible and watch campmeeting DVDs we purchased for him to enjoy and DVDs of Don F. of our beliefs. We had family worships together and prayed together. We purchased pretty religious music CDs for Jonathan to listen to and enjoy. We had our own campmeetings together and pretty music with sing-spiration times. We did all we could to win Jonathan back to wanting

> *We did all we could to win Jonathan back to wanting to love and obey Jesus and follow Jesus with all his heart. But the time finally came when Jonathan decided he wanted to return back to the care center and leave home and do what he wanted to do*

to love and obey Jesus and follow Jesus with all his heart. But the time finally came when Jonathan decided he wanted to return back to the care center and leave home and do what he wanted to do. God's unseen hand is still in control of the situation and only God knows the outcome of it all. It's all in God's hands! Only God sees the future and only He knows the rest of this story and the plans God has for our son Jonathan. We still continue to pray and claim Proverbs 22:6, "Train up a child in the way he should go: and when he is old, he will not depart from it". God is still guiding, directing and planning and protecting. Proverbs 16:9, "A man's heart deviseth his way: but the Lord directeth his steps."

In *Last Day Events* by E.G. White, she has this to say on p. 29, "In the great closing work, we shall meet with perplexities that we know not how to deal with, but let us not forget that the three great powers of heaven are working, that a divine hand is on the wheel, and that God will bring His purposes to pass. As the wheel-like complications were under the guidance of the hand beneath the wings of the cherubim, so the complicated play of human events is under divine control. Amidst the strife and tumult of nations, He that sitteth above the cherubim still guides the affairs of the earth."

In book 2 of *Selected Messages* by E.G. White, she gives us these comforting words, "The Holy One of Israel, who calls the host of heaven by name, and holds the stars of heaven in position, has you individually in His keeping…" Right now we may not know the outcome for Jonathan's life and how the Lord will reach his heart and mind to depart from Satan and these bad habits. But we have faith to know God has a thousand ways to provide for us of which we know nothing. Read this in *Ministry of Healing* by E.G. White pp. 481 and 482. She also says, "Worry is blind and cannot discern the future, but Jesus sees the end from the beginning. In every difficulty He has His way prepared to bring relief… His love is as far above all other love as the heavens above the earth. He watches over His children with a love that is measureless and everlasting. In the darkest days, when appearances seems most forbidding, have faith in God. He is working out His will, doing all things well in behalf of his people." Romans 8:28, "And we know that all things work together for good to them that love God, to them who are the called according to his purpose."

Psalm 105:1, "O give thanks unto the LORD; call upon his name: make known his deeds among the people."

By faith we see God's unseen hand in control and keep praying and claiming God's promises like: Jeremiah 29:11–14, "For I know the thoughts that I think toward you, saith the Lord, thoughts of peace, and not of evil, to give you an expected end. Then shall ye call upon me, and ye shall go and pray unto me, and I will hearken unto you. And ye shall seek me, and find me, when ye shall search for me with all your heart. And I will be found of you, saith the Lord: and I will turn away your captivity, and I will gather you from all the nations, and from all the places whether I have driven you, saith the Lord; and I will bring you again into the place whence I caused you to be carried away captive."

Isaiah 43:1–3, "But now thus saith the LORD that created thee, O Jacob, and he that formed thee, O Israel, Fear not: for I have redeemed thee, I have called thee by thy name; thou art mine. When thou passest through the waters, I will be with thee; and through the rivers, they shall not overflow thee: when thou walkest through the fire, thou shalt not be burned; neither shall the flame kindle upon thee. For I am the LORD thy God, the Holy One of Israel, thy Saviour: I gave Egypt for thy ransom, Ethiopia and Seba for thee." Read also, Psalm 139.

Isaiah 41:10, 13, "Fear thou not; for I am with thee: be not dismayed; for I am thy God: I will strengthen thee; yea, I will help thee; yea, I will uphold thee with the right hand of my righteousness… For I the LORD thy God will hold thy right hand, saying unto thee, Fear not; I will help thee."

We may not know, at this time, what God may choose to do to get Jonathan's attention to get him back on the straight and narrow path that leads to heaven. Matthew 7:13, 14. We do know God has His unseen hand directing and guiding in all that's being done and God loves Jonathan, even more than we, his parents, love him. God has plans for Jonathan, otherwise He would never have spared his life so very many times, so Jonathan could come to his senses and change his ways and be saved and win souls for Jesus.

In the Bible we read the story of King Nebuchadnezzar in Daniel 4, and how the Lord allowed him to eat grass like an animal in the fields for seven years until he acknowledged God as the Ruler in control over him and his kingdom.

Read the book of Jonah in the Bible and how God had to allow Jonah to go through the experience in the whale's belly to get Jonah to do what God wanted him to do.

Then there was Saul, who met Christ on the road to Damascus, when there shone a light from heaven and knocked him to the ground and he heard a voice saying, "Saul, Saul, why persecutest thou me?" And he said, who art thou, Lord? And the Lord said, I am Jesus whom thou persecutest: it is hard for thee to kick against the pricks. And he trembling and astonished said, Lord, what wilt thou have me to do? And the Lord said unto him, Arise, and go into the city, and it shall be told thee what though must do…" Continue to read the whole story in Acts 9:1–31. God had a plan for Saul. He changed his name to Paul and he became a great missionary and a great soul winner for Jesus.

Then, we have Peter, the disciple of Jesus who walked with God, but then he denied his Lord at Jesus' trial three times. This broke Peter's heart and he wept bitterly. But from then on, Peter determined to serve his Master with all his heart and stands boldly for Jesus and His cause until the end. Read his experience in Matthew 26:57–75.

Then we have the demoniac who was changed and in his right mind when Jesus touched him and made something beautiful out of his life for Jesus. He became the first missionary Jesus sent out to witness for Him. Read the whole story in Mark 5:1–20, especially verses 18–20, "And when he was come into the ship, he that had been possessed with the devil prayed him that he might be with him. Howbeit Jesus suffered him not, but saith unto him, Go home to thy friends, and tell them how great things the Lord hath done for thee, and hath had compassion on thee. And he departed, and began to publish in Decapolis how great things Jesus had done for him: and all men did marvel."

Jonathan, in the two and a half years, he was here with us said one day, after we had rolled him in his wheelchair to go see a cabin we had just finished building and had it all done and painted and furnished and the rug down, he said when he saw it, "I like it here! I want to live in this cabin! I want to be your first missionary!" Praise the Lord! Jonathan was listening to the Holy Spirit then speaking to his heart. We just continue to pray that he will listen to the Holy Spirit and change his mind and not want to go back to his old lifestyle of sinful pleasures in the care center he wants to go to when he's dismissed from the hospital, where he's at getting his depression cared for. While he was 11 days in the hospital, we sent out S.O.S. requests for prayer for Jonathan! We prayed he wouldn't end up in a care center going back to his old sinful pleasures, but that God would please place His unseen hand on Jonathan and bring him back home where he could get the help he needed in the Lord. God did place His unseen hand on Jonathan, and brought him back home from the hospital! Praise the Lord! Thank you Jesus!

While at the hospital they put Jonathan on a lot of drugs and raised the doses of his other drugs. He came home all drugged up! But we were so thankful at least he was back home, where we could still try and encourage him in the Lord. God had again overruled Satan and heard all of our prayers for Jonathan to keep him out of a nursing home, where he was planning on going back to his old flunky lifestyle again! God has given us a little more time to work with Jonathan. Only God sees and knows the future, as God's unseen hand is still guiding and directing in all that's happening. We claim Matthew 21:22, "And all things, whatsoever ye shall ask in prayer, believing, ye shall receive."

We have faith that God is still in control of the situation and will see Jonathan and us through it all in his own way and time. Soon Christ is to come and end all this heartache and misery and pain and sorrow and trials and trouble. We just want to be ready and help Jonathan and others to be ready. We need to be listening to the voice of God saying to us in Isaiah 30:20, 21, "And though the Lord give you the bread of adversity, and the water of affliction, yet shall not thy teachers be removed into a corner any more, but thine eyes shall see thy teachers: And thine ears shall hear a word behind thee, saying, This is the way, walk ye in it, when ye turn to the right hand, and when ye turn to the left." In John 14:6, "Jesus saith unto him, I am the way, the truth, and the life: no man cometh unto the Father, but by me."

In *3T* by E.G. White on p. 380, she asks these serious questions and comments on them, "Will you, young friends, arise and shake off this dreadful indifference and stupor which has conformed you to the world? Will you heed the voice of warning which tells you that destruction lies in the path of those who are at ease in this hour of danger? God's patience will not always wait for you, poor, trifling souls. He who holds our destinies in His hands will not always be trifled with. Jesus declares to us that there is a greater sin than that which caused the destruction of Sodom and Gomorrah. It is the sin of those who have the great light of truth in these days and who are not moved to repentance. It is the sin of rejecting the light of the most solemn message of mercy to the world. It is the sin of those who see Jesus in the wilderness of temptation, bowed down as with mortal agony because of the sins of the world, and yet are not moved to thorough repentance. He fasted nearly six weeks to overcome, in behalf of men, the indulgence of appetite and vanity, and the desire for display and worldly honor. He has shown them how they may overcome on their own account as He overcame; but it is not pleasant to their natures to endure conflict and reproach, derision and shame, for His dear sake. It is not agreeable to deny self and to be ever seeking to do good to others. It is not pleasant to overcome as Christ overcame, so they turn from the pattern which is plainly given them to copy and refuse to imitate the example that the Saviour came from the heavenly courts to leave them. It shall be more tolerable for Sodom and Gomorrah in the day of judgment than for those who have had the privileges and the great light which shines in our day, but who have neglected to follow the light and to give their hearts fully to God."

When Jonathan came home this time from his hospital stay for his depression, he said he was going to stay home with us and not go into a care center! We just praised the Lord for helping Jonathan to make this decision and not want to go back to his old sinful lifestyle in a nursing home facility! Thank you Jesus for answering our prayers moving Jonathan to make this decision, by your unseen hand! We give God all the glory for what He is doing and for all He has done to keep Jonathan alive and working on his heart to come back home and back to the God he loves. Jonathan made the remark while we were having worship, "I love Jesus. I have faith in Him. God is helping me." That's music to our ears. We have faith and hope God will help us, as a family, to make it to heaven together!

> *We give God all the glory for what He is doing and for all He has done to keep Jonathan alive and working on his heart to come back home and back to the God he loves*

Sister White says in *Gospel Workers* pp. 514–519, "Many are God's promises to those who minister to His afflicted ones. He says: "Blessed is he that considereth the poor: the Lord will deliver him in time of trouble. The Lord will preserve him, and keep him alive; and he shall be blessed upon the earth: and Thou wilt not deliver him unto the will of his enemies. The Lord will strengthen him upon the bed of languishing: Thou wilt make all his bed in his sickness.… While much of the fruit of their labor is not apparent in this life, God's workers have His sure promise of ultimate success. As the world's Redeemer, Christ was constantly confronted with apparent failure. He seemed to do little of the work which He longed to do in uplifting and saving. Satanic agencies were constantly working to obstruct His way. But He would not be discouraged. Ever before Him He saw the result of His mission. He knew that truth would finally triumph in the contest with evil, and to His disciples He said: "These things I have spoken unto you, that in Me ye might have peace. In the world ye shall have tribulation: but be of good cheer; I have overcome the world." John 16:33. The life of Christ's disciples is to be like His, a series of uninterrupted victories—not seen to be such here, but recognized as such in the great hereafter. Those who labor for the good of others are working in union with the heavenly angels. They have their constant companionship, their unceasing ministry. Angels of light and power are ever near to protect, to comfort, to heal, to instruct, to inspire. The highest education, the truest culture, the most exalted service possible to human beings in this world, are theirs.

Often our merciful Father encourages His children and strengthens their faith by permitting them here to see evidence of the power of His grace upon the hearts and lives of those for whom they labor… Christ delights to take apparently hopeless material, those whom Satan has debased and through whom he has worked, and make them the subjects of His grace. He rejoices to deliver them from suffering, and from the wrath that is to fall upon the disobedient. He makes His children His agents in the accomplishment of this work, and in its success, even in this life, they find a precious reward. It is still with His struggling children on earth, who have the battle with the destroyer yet to wage. "Father," He says, "I will that they also, whom Thou hast given Me, be with Me where I am." Christ's redeemed ones are His jewels, His precious and peculiar treasure… And will not His workers rejoice when they, too, behold the fruit of their labors?… Every impulse of the Holy Spirit leading men to goodness and to God, is noted in the books of heaven, and in the day of God every one who has given himself as an instrument for the Holy Spirit's working, will be permitted to behold what his life has wrought. Wonderful will be the revealing as the lines of holy influence, with their precious results, are brought to view. What will be the gratitude of souls that will meet us in the heavenly courts, as they understand the sympathetic, loving interest which has been taken in their salvation!

All praise, honor, and glory will be given to God and to the Lamb for our redemption; but it will not detract from the glory of God to express gratitude to the instrumentality He has employed in the salvation of souls ready to perish. The redeemed will meet and recognize those whose attention they have directed to the uplifted Saviour. What blessed converse they will have with these souls! "I was a sinner," it will be said, "without God and without hope in the world; and you came to me, and drew my attention to the precious Saviour as my only hope. And I believed in Him. I repented of my sins, and was made to sit together with His saints in heavenly places in Christ Jesus"… I demolished my idols, and worshiped God, and now I see Him face to face… "When despair bound my soul in unbelief, the Lord sent you to me," they say, "to speak words of hope and comfort. You brought me food for my physical necessities, and you opened to me the word of God, awakening me to my spiritual needs. You treated me as a brother. You sympathized with me in my sorrows, and restored my bruised and wounded soul, so that I could grasp the hand of Christ that was reached out to save me. In my ignorance you taught me patiently that I had a Father in heaven who cared for me. You read to me the precious promises of God's word. You inspired in me faith that He would save me. My heart was softened, subdued, broken, as I contemplated the sacrifice which Christ had made for me. I became hungry for the bread of life, and the truth was precious to my soul. I am here, saved, eternally saved, ever to live in His presence, and to praise Him who gave His life for me." What rejoicing there will be as these redeemed ones meet and greet those who have had a burden in their behalf! And those who have lived, not to please themselves, but to be a blessing to the unfortunate who have so few blessings—how their hearts will thrill with satisfaction! They will realize the promise, "Thou shalt be blessed; for they cannot recompense thee: for thou shalt be recompensed at the resurrection of the just."

Jonathan made this comment to me when he came home from the hospital, "You and dad have done so much for me, I really do appreciate it! I really do love you and dad. Thanks for the letter you wrote me while I was in the hospital." I said, "We really do love you too, and we're so happy and thankful you chose to come back home and stay with us! God will help you! We did a lot of praying for you and a lot of people were praying for you too!" I gave him a hug and a kiss and he hugged me and kissed me too. While Jonathan was in the hospital and we were doing a lot of praying and fasting, dad saw out his bedroom window two red birds in the bush. David and I were encouraged by this sign that God was near and hearing our prayers and the others praying for Jonathan too. Dad and I feel God is near when we see the red bird. This is a sign we chose when dad would go canvassing and would ask God to send the red bird to direct him to someone who would buy a book and sure enough as he prayed, God would send a red bird to direct him to a home where the people there would buy a book or two! Praise the Lord! We also praised the Lord for the encouraging words we were hearing Jonathan speak to us when he got home from the hospital. We're all so happy to be back together again as a family and praising God for His unseen hand upon us.

There's one more experience I want to share of God's unseen hand upon us. One time when we drove to go see Jonathan when he was away at school. On our trip back home several miles from home, the front tire on the car began to wobble and was loose and looked like it would fall off! There was nothing we could do to fix it and all we could do was pray for God to help us make it home safe and keep the wheel on the car! He had to drive real slow as we wobbled down the highway praying and trusting the Lord to keep the tire on until we could make it safely home. As we crossed a bridge, some construction workers shouted, "Your front tire is coming off!" We said, "Thank you, we know it!" Then we just kept driving slowly on by as the workers just gazed in amazement as we kept driving the car with the front tire loose and wobbling all over. We finally made it safely home and as we pulled into our driveway, the tire fell off! But we were okay. Something had broken loose under the car but the angel kept the tire on until we got safely home in our driveway!

Truly God's unseen hand was there protecting us and kept us from an accident by keeping our tire on our car! Praise the Lord! Thank you Jesus! Just another way God tested our faith and trust in Him to see us through this terrible and horrifying and dangerous experience. God allowed us to go through, so our faith in Him would grow!

The following letter is what I wrote and sent to Jonathan while he was in the hospital October 1 to 11, 2016.

October 3, 2016

I hope your heart pains have gone away! And also your shoulder and arm pains are gone! Don't want you to have a heart attack! Proverbs 22:6; Isaiah 41:10, 13; Psalm 121.

My dear and precious son, Jonathan,

Dad and I sure do miss you! Things are so quiet around the house. We love you and are praying for you and hope you will soon be well! Remember, Jesus loves you and has plans for you! Keep close to Jesus! He's carrying you in His arms of love like the poem, "Footprints in the Sand" says. Jesus is soon to come and end all our pain and sorrow and heartaches! Dad and I want to be with you in heaven! With God's help we'll make it, just hang in there and never give up! Keep fighting the good fight of faith! 1 Timothy 6:12. I wish I could talk to you!! I wish I could see you!! Our old truck is in a bad way and dangerous to drive! Our car is still in the shop, and have no idea when we'll get it back! You're in our prayers and thoughts! We're praying you'll make the right decision where you want to go when you're dismissed! It's all in God's hands! God is stronger than Satan! I'm still writing on my story: "God's Unseen Hand". What you're going through right now is just another time God's unseen hand is watching over you and guiding you and protecting you! Things will all turn out okay as you let God have control of your life and surrender your all to Jesus! We're so proud of you! You've come a long way in the two and a half years you've been home with us! Don't give up now! You'll win in the race of life if you don't give up! You have God on your side and parents who love you and want to see you well and happy in the LORD! Keep counting your blessings! God has seen you through so much and He won't fail you now! Have faith in God! Hebrews 11. God bless you and keep you in His tender loving care! We love you!!! Love, MOM & DAD xoxoxo

P.S. <u>Please</u> drop us a line how you're doing and what you plan to do! <u>Please</u> let the nurses know to drop us a line letting us know what's going on, since they can't call us, since we have no phone and no vehicle to come up there! Thanks! I've enclosed a stamped envelope and paper for you to <u>please</u> notify me of where you choose to go when you're dismissed! I don't want to lose track of where you are!! Thanks! <u>Please</u> take care of yourself! We don't want to lose you!!!!

While Jonathan was in the hospital they had put him on a lot of new drugs and high doses and raised the doses of his other drugs he was on. They had put him on a high dose of pain medicine for a pain he had in his right arm. All these drugs were messing him up and he wasn't doing very well. He started getting off his pain pills and was having a terribly hard time. Several of the drugs they put him on in the hospital were causing his blood sugar to go up high, and he had gained a lot of weight while in the hospital and his legs and feet were terribly swollen, and one of the side effects was shortness of breath and another side effect was panic attacks. He felt so very tired and weak as all these drugs were poisoning his system. Other side effects he was feeling were anxiety and depression. One of the drugs he was on had a side effect of sudden death! He was trying to cope with all these terrible drugs he was put on but feeling worse and worse. Jonathan decided to come back home and get help. He'd try and relax in his easy chair and listen to some pretty religious music to try and sooth his nerves. There are two songs he especially liked to listen to and they are: "One Pair of Hands" and the other song was "He Knows Our Names."

We know God's unseen hand is upon Jonathan helping him through all he's going through. Then about two o'clock in the morning Jonathan woke me up and said, "I'm so depressed and I can't get my breath!" I said, "Did you use your breathing machine to see if that will help you get your breath?" He said, "Yes! But it's not helping any!" I stayed up with him and had prayer with him and read the Bible to him. Nothing seemed to help his depression, and his breathing was getting more labored! He finally said, "I've got to go to the Emergency room!" It was around 3:00 a.m. and dad hurried him into the Emergency room in Ottawa. They admitted him to the hospital and Jonathan said he didn't want to go back home, but be put in a care center when he was dismissed from the hospital. Dad had prayer with him and then came on back home and we prayed for him all through the night. The next day dad drove over to the hospital to see how he was doing. I didn't go because our old truck has a blown engine and the engine noise is getting worse and worse, so I fixed up a little fruit and food basket and picked a pretty two-colored rose flower and put it in a little vase and wrote a little note on it telling him mom and dad love you and Jesus loves you, and we're praying for you and may you get well soon and God bless you! John 3:16.

I got his bundle of clothes ready for him to have to go with him when they dismissed him to wherever he was going to go, since he didn't want to return back home. I knew God's unseen hand was upon him and would be with him wherever he went. I claimed the promise in Joshua 1:9, "Have not I commanded thee? Be strong and of a good courage; be not afraid, neither be thou dismayed: for the Lord thy God is with thee whithersoever thou goest." I had to show faith and trust that the good Lord would take care of him in his folly and spare his life and give him more time to be converted. Before dad left home to go see how Jonathan was doing and take his clothes up to him, we had prayer together and prayed dad would have a safe trip up there and back in our old dangerous broken down truck he had to drive in an emergency, since our old 1998 Honda car had so much wrong with it and it was in the shop being repaired. We prayed dad would find Jonathan doing okay too. I knew God's unseen hand had to be with dad too, in our old junky truck!

Dad found Jonathan doing okay and sleeping comfortably in bed. The nurses said he's doing better, but at this time they're not sure where he'll be going when he's completely well. He needs to be in a facility to be able to take care of all his needs and regulate all the different medicines he's on. Jonathan woke up to enjoy a little visit with his dad and then fell back asleep again. Dad had prayer with him before he left and explained to the nurses that we had no phone and for them to drop us a line and let us know where he'd be going from the hospital. They said okay and for dad to leave Jonathan's bundle of clothes in his room. Jonathan knows dad and I are so against him wanting to stay on these terribly dangerous and deadly drugs and we don't want him taking them here, because they're making him get worse instead of better. So, he wants to go to a place where he can keep taking all these drugs the doctors put him on while in the hospital the first time around. And we can't help him get well when he's so drugged up and can't think or reason right and all these drugs are poisoning him and taking the life and strength out of him and making him tired and weak and don't feel like existing and can't move around very well. It's so sad too, to see all the bad side effects he's suffering from on all these bad drugs. But he prefers to go somewhere else, other than home, to be able to stay on them. All we can do is pray and ask God to keep His unseen hand upon him and guide and direct and provide and heal and convert him. While dad was gone taking Jonathan to the emergency room at 3:00 a.m. when he was depressed and couldn't get his breath, they had admitted him to the hospital. I was home praying for him and for their safety in our old pick-up truck with the blown engine. While I prayed and read my Bible, I fell asleep and dreamed about a little lost sheep. It inspired me to write the following poem, "The One Lost Sheep," that explained the dream I had.

I also dreamed I was saying, "Cut loose from the cords that bind you." Proverbs 5:22.

Another dream I had was I was saying this in my dream, "The curse causeless shall not come." Proverbs 26:2. The same time, I dreamt this dream:

In my dream I was saying to someone, (it could have been Jonathan) "Come to Jesus just as you are." Matthew 11:28-30; Isaiah 1:18. It makes me think of the song, "Just As I Am." (Read *Steps to Christ* book by E.G. White). I dreamt this text too, 2 Timothy 3:12. I was quoting it in my dream. The next night while Jonathan was still in the hospital, I dreamt this dream. It was a song entitled, "Put Your Hand in the Hand."

This same night I dreamed this following dream two times on the same night: I heard a voice in my dream saying, "Saul, Saul, why persecutest thou me? I am Jesus whom thou persecutest: it is hard for thee to kick against the pricks." Acts 9:4, 5. (Read all Acts 9).

(It's like Jonathan kicking against the pricks wanting to do what he wants to do and not what God wants him to do.)

Jonathan reminds me of the prodigal son. The story is found in Luke 15:11-32. Jonathan wants to leave home and go off to somewhere where he can eat, drink and be merry and live a reckless wasted life in riotous living and not stay home and abide by the rules and regulations at home.

With its restrictions and restraints. We keep praying for him. Just nine hours before we had to take Jonathan to the Emergency room because he couldn't get his breath and because he was feeling depressed, I was out running around our circle driveway, and I looked up in the sky, and I saw a big mammoth cloud formation of a bird covering over one-third of our land on the "Ark". It made me think of the RED BIRD God uses to sometimes communicate with us. This bird-cloud formation looked just like the picture of the red bird I drew and put on my story I wrote, "A Red Bird Answers Our Prayer."

This is exactly how it looked with the beak and the eye and its wings spread out and the feet stretched out. I believe God put that cloud formation of the red bird in the sky to remind me, "God is near!" Dad and I decided years ago that whenever we'd see a red bird we'd feel like God was telling us He's near! Like when David would canvass and wasn't making any sales, he'd pray and ask God to <u>please</u> send a red bird to lead him to a home where someone would buy a book. Then a red bird would come in answer to his prayer, and would fly directly in front of him and would go down the street and turn up another street and then at the house the people were home, the bird would disappear and they would buy a book or two! This has happened several times!

Right now, while we've been going through some rough times with Jonathan, our son, sick and he'd been in the hospital, this cloud formation of our red bird was comforting to see the exact bird I drew on my "Red Bird" story, was reproduced in the clouds to remind me of God's presence and His unseen hand was over all, and He was still in control of things going on in our life, and He was watching over us and our son, Jonathan. I just praised the Lord and thanked Him for doing this for me! God can do anything! Luke 1:37 and Mark 10:27. I also like Romans 8:28, "And we know that all things work together for good to them that love God, to them who are the called according to his purpose."

We also still keep claiming Proverbs 22:6 for Jonathan. We have raised and trained Jonathan for the Lord, and he's our investment project, and we pray God will make something beautiful of Jonathan's life for God's glory, however He chooses to do it and whenever He chooses to do it!

As Jonathan continues to recuperate in the hospital, where God's unseen hand watches over him, it makes me think of an experience we had. It was a couple of months ago. We had been told by the weather station radio that there was a 70% chance of a severe storm with strong damaging winds and heavy rains to hit our area during the night. We prayed before we went to bed that night that God would please send the angel of the Lord to encamp round about us and protect us and deliver us, as Psalm 34:6-8 promises to do. The electricity went off a couple of times during the night and we kept praying it would please come back on and it did! Thank you Jesus! God's unseen hand was over us and taking care of us through the storm! Then the next morning when I went out to walk around our circle driveway and talk to the Lord and thank Him for looking after us and the "Ark" during this bad storm, I looked up in the sky and I saw this BIG gigantic enormous phenomenal cloud formation in the shape of a right human hand extended out over our little "Ark". Like the Lord's BIG right hand covering over our dwelling place to shelter us from the storms passing by, so we were protected in the hollow of His strong and loving and caring hands!

Like Isaiah 41:10 and 13 says, "Fear thou not; for I am with thee: be not dismayed; for I am thy God: I will strengthen thee; yea, I will help thee; yea, I will uphold thee with the right hand of my righteousness... For I the LORD thy God will hold thy right hand, saying unto thee, Fear not; I will help thee." What an awe-inspiring phenomenal thing to behold! God had truly been watching over us through the night in this terrible storm. There was no damage to anything! In our worship that morning we had thanked and praised God for His tender loving care over us and the "Ark". It made me realize how God will take care of us and protect us and supply all our needs in the early and the great time of trouble ahead of us, as we remain faithful to Jesus and His 7th day Sabbath and all His 10 Commandments. Truly God's unseen hand had been placed over us in the time of storm. It makes me think of the song, "A Shelter in the Time of Storm", and the promises God gives us in Psalm 91; Psalm 46; Psalm 40; Psalm 56:3, "What time I am afraid, I will trust in thee." Also the promise in Isaiah 33:15, 16, 17. Read *Desire of Ages* by E.G. White, pp. 667–669 the chapter, "Let Not Your Heart Be Troubled."

While Jonathan was in the hospital getting well, he was deciding if he wanted to go to the care center when dismissed from the hospital and not come back home. We had been doing a lot of praying and fasting that he would decide to come back home and not end up in the devil's trap going back to his old lifestyle in the care center. The very day Jonathan made his decision to come back home when dismissed from the hospital, unbeknownst to us, was the very day I was outside working with daddy on the electrical line on the 12' x 20' cabin we had just bought, and as I walked by our house trailer, I heard Jonathan's voice crying out in a desperate call for help saying "MOM!" I heard his voice calling from inside the house trailer! I thought, "Jonathan is in the hospital, not in the house trailer!" But I heard it clearly, and it was definitely his voice crying out for help! Dad and I prayed for him that he'd be doing okay and that he'd decide to come on home and not listen to Satan to go back to the care center and his old life of sin! The very next day, the hospital's transportation car drove in our driveway with Jonathan coming home to stay! Praise the Lord! He had decided to come on home the very day I heard his voice calling, "MOM!" We were so very happy and thankful to see him back home again and to stay! We thanked the good Lord for hearing our earnest prayers for Jonathan to decide to come back home! We thanked the transportation man from the hospital for bringing our son, Jonathan back home to us! Jonathan said he was cutting out some of those drugs he had been put on and was going to cut down the doses on his other medicines he was on. We were so thankful for that because he was having so many side effects from all those drugs the doctor at the hospital had put him on. We were so proud of him and his decision to come back home and not go back to his old habits in the care center! We just praised the Lord and thanked Him and gave Jonathan hugs and kisses. It was so good to be a family together again! God's unseen hand had overruled Satan's attempt to lure Jonathan back to his old ways again! Thank you Jesus! Jesus is stronger than Satan. Jonathan had listened to Jesus and came back home where he was loved and needed and where he was free of Satan's traps set for him in the care center. Jesus had defeated Satan and spared Jonathan's life again! Praise the Lord! Read Jude 24; Matthew 21:22; Jeremiah 33:3; Philippians 4:13.

Jonathan said that he's not depressed or short of breath, and he's feeling better getting off all those many drugs they had him on! God is good! May Jonathan continue his journey of life staying safely in God's unseen hands. And fulfill the plan God has for his life as He cooperates with God. *Ministry of Healing* p. 476. God gave me this song in a dream: "Shepherd of Love".

P.S. Jeremiah 29:11-13. As I finished writing this story, God gave me this dream: "God has a plan for each person's life." Read "Ministry of Healing" by E.G. White pp. 469-482 "Help in Daily Living" chapter. We claim Isaiah 59:1.

The following poem and story were written from a dream I had on October 22, 2016 about "The One Lost Sheep". Makes me think of the songs, "The Ninety and Nine" and "Rescue the Perishing" and "Softly and Tenderly". Proverbs 22:6; Luke 15; Isaiah 53; John 3:16; *Christ's Object Lessons* by E.G. White pp. 186–192 "The Lost Sheep"; *Last Day Events* by E.G. White, p. 211.

God gave me this song in a dream: "Shepherd of Love".

Linda Clore's dream about "The One Lost Sheep."
October 22, 2016

In my dream I was seeing this:

A little lost sheep had strayed from the fold and got lost in the mountains out in the wilds and the cold. The good Shepherd left the comforts of His home and went searching and hunting for His one lost sheep out in the wilds and in the cold, lost and hurt and frightened. The good Shepherd went all through the night and all through the mountains and all through the cold and all through the dangers, calling and trying to find and rescue His one little lost sheep. He finally heard the sheep's faint cry and when He had found him stuck in the thorns and thicket, hurt and bleeding, He picked him up in his own hurt and torn and bleeding hands and feet and carried the little lost sheep in His loving arms and on His shoulders safely back to the fold with the other ninety and nine sheep. There the good Shepherd tenderly cared for his little lost sheep's needs by cleaning him up and feeding him and lovingly bound up his wounds. But this terrible ordeal, the good Shepherd had to go through to save His one lost sheep, He loved so much, cost the life of the good Shepherd.

This made me think of the songs, "The Ninety and Nine" and "Rescue the Perishing". It also made me think of our son, Jonathan, and the sinner who strays from Jesus and goes out into the cold cruel world, lost and sad and lonely and how Jesus comes searching for him and finds him all hurt and bruised and brings him safely back to the fold and cares for his needs. But it cost the life of Jesus, our good Shepherd, to be able to rescue this one lost sinner. But there was such great joy the lost sheep was found! (Read *Christ's Object Lessons* by E.G. White pp. 186–192, "The Lost Sheep". Isaiah 53; John 3:16.)

In the *Last Day Events* book by E.G. White, she says, "Many who have strayed from the fold will come back to follow the great Shepherd." On p. 187, in *Christ's Object Lessons*, Sister White makes this comment, "In the parable the shepherd goes out to search for one sheep – the very least that can be numbered. So, if there had been but one lost soul, Christ would have died for that one." On p. 190 she continues saying, "By the lost sheep, Christ represents not only the individual sinner but the one world that has apostatized and has been ruined by sin. This world is but an atom in the vast dominion over which God presides, yet this little fallen world—the one lost sheep—is more precious in His sight than are the ninety and nine that went not astray from the fold."

God impressed me to write the following poem, "The One Lost Sheep," when I had this dream about "The One Lost Sheep" on October 22, 2016.

"THE ONE LOST SHEEP"
Written by Linda Clore
October 22, 2016

A little lost sheep had strayed from the fold.
Got lost out in the wilds and in the cold.
The good Shepherd left the comforts of Home,
To find His lost sheep that had from Him roamed.
Never giving up, He heard the faint cry,
Coming from His lost sheep, ready to die!
Though tired and bleeding, He rescued him!
Jesus finds us and saves us from our sins.
All we like the lost sheep have gone astray.

All we like the lost sheep have disobeyed.
Jesus reaches out with His loving arms,
And carries us home from dangers and harm.
Back to the fold and the ninety and nine,
There safe from Satan and cared for and fine.
But this ordeal cost the good Shepherd's life,
To suffer and bleed to save the sheep's life!
What more could Jesus have done to save us?
He left all Heaven and died to save us!
We should be willing to part with our sins,
And then trust our life and keeping to Him.
But too many times we want it our way.
Like the little lost sheep, we go astray.
It cost so much to bring us back again.
And some lost sheep never come back again!
Oh! What a terrible thought to be lost!
To lose out on Heaven and what it cost!
Let's surrender all to Jesus right now!
Let's be determined to be saved right now!
Give up this world and its pleasures of sin.
Be determined to never sin again!
Jesus loves you and wants you to be saved.
Give your heart to Jesus without delay!
Jesus wants to carry you to Heaven,
And enter those pearly gates in Heaven.
That decision is up to you and me.
Come to Him, as you are, and be set free!
And like the lost sheep, come back to the fold,
And the smiling face of Jesus behold!
Make the good Shepherd rejoice in Heaven,
Cause you've come back and have chosen Heaven!

(Read *Desire of Ages* by E.G. White, chapter 52, "The Divine Shepherd". Especially read pp. 479–480, "Jesus knows us individually, and is touched with the feeling of our infirmities. He knows us all by name... Every soul is as fully known to Jesus as if he were the only one for whom the Saviour died. The distress of every one touches His heart. The cry for aid reaches His ear... He cares for each one as if there were not another on the face of the earth... Today the same tender, sympathizing heart is open to all the woes of humanity. Today the hand that was pierced is reached forth to bless more abundantly His people that are in the world. 'And they shall never perish, neither shall any man pluck them out of My hand.'" (Read John 10:16, 27-29). Also, on p. 483 Sister White writes, "The soul that has given himself to Christ is more precious in His sight than the whole world. The Saviour would have passed through the agony of Calvary that one might be saved in His kingdom. He will never abandon one for whom He has died. Unless His followers choose to leave Him, He will hold them fast. Through all our trials we have a never-failing Helper. He does not leave us alone to struggle with temptation, to battle with evil, and be finally crushed with burdens and sorrow. Though now He is hidden from mortal sight, the ear of faith can hear His voice saying, Fear not; I am with you... I know your tears; I also have wept. The griefs that lie too deep to be breathed into any human ear, I know. Think not that you are desolate and forsaken. Though your pain touch no responsive chord in any heart on earth, look unto Me, and live. (Read Isaiah 54:10). Because we are the gift of His Father, and the reward of His work, Jesus loves us. He loves us as His children. Reader, He loves you. Heaven itself can bestow nothing greater, nothing better. Therefore trust."

Read also *5 Testimonies for the Church* by E.G. White, p 754, "The tireless vigilance of the heavenly messengers, and their unceasing employment in their ministry in connection with the beings of earth, show us how God's hand is guiding the wheel within a wheel. (Ezekiel 10:8–10) ... He (God) will work with them if they will put away iniquity and become pure in heart and life... That which appears to finite minds entangled and complicated, the Lord's hand can keep in perfect order... He who ruleth in the heavens is our Saviour. He measures every trial. He watches the furnace fire..." God will not give us any more than we can bear. Read 1 Corinthians 10:13.

Like when Jonathan was in the hospital this last time because he couldn't get his breath, he was having bad side effects from all the drugs he had been put on and he was holding fluids in his lungs and legs and the right side of his heart was acting up. They gave him inhalation therapy. God was holding Jonathan up in His unseen hand, sparing his life, giving him more time to be saved. He recovered when he came home and got off a lot of these many drugs he was on, causing so much trouble. His lungs cleared up and his fluid retention stopped and he could breathe okay and then the swelling in his legs went away and he felt his strength coming back. Praise the Lord! Thank you Jesus! Sister White says in *Last Day Events* p. 151, "But we may trust our hand in the hand of Christ amid darkness and peril".

One night, while writing on my story about Jonathan, "God's Unseen Hand", God gave me a dream and I saw written out these words, "God's Unseen Hand." In the same night, for the second time, I saw, "God's Unseen Hand", the story of Jonathan in my dream. I saw him in my dream getting into his herbs and medicine drawer. God is watching and seeing all that is going on and "God's Unseen Hand" is watching over Jonathan and helping him in all he's doing and taking care of him and protecting him from Satan's temptations and traps, as God is working on his life to save him and give him salvation and victory in his life. Praise God! Thank you Jesus!

May God bless each of you in your journey with God, as you realize "God's Unseen Hand" is upon you and guiding and directing and protecting you and providing for you, as you walk and work for Jesus and prepare for the future when the Sunday Law Crises will be upon us, and we'll need Jesus to care for us and help us make the right decisions to follow Him and do His will and trust Him to see us through the trials and hardships ahead of us, as we surrender all to Jesus. Sister White writes in *Steps to Christ* in the chapter, "The Privilege of Prayer", p. 96, "Through sincere prayer we are brought into connection with the mind of the Infinite. We may have no remarkable evidence at the time that the face of our Redeemer is bending over us in compassion and love, but this is even so. We may not feel His visible touch, but His hand is upon us in love and pitying tenderness." Also, on p. 103 we read, "We should keep in our thoughts every blessing we receive from God, and when we realize His great love we should be willing to trust everything to the hand that was nailed to the cross for us."

> *May God bless each of you in your journey with God, as you realize "God's Unseen Hand" is upon you and guiding and directing and protecting you and providing for you, as you walk and work for Jesus and prepare for the future*

In *Ministry of Healing* by Sister White, we read on p. 513, "The result of all we do rests in the hands of God. Whatever may betide, lay hold upon Him with steady, persevering confidence." She also says on p. 509, "Prayer and faith will do what no power on earth can accomplish... Christ is ever sending messages to those who listen for His voice."

I like Sister White's quote in *Steps to Christ* on pp. 66, 69 and 70, "When we do not receive the very things we ask for, at the time we ask, we are still to believe that the Lord hears, and that He will answer our prayers... Keep your wants, your joys, your sorrows, your cares and your fears, before God. You cannot burden Him; you cannot weary Him. He who numbers the hairs of your head is not indifferent to the wants of His children... Take to Him everything that perplexes the mind. Nothing is too great for Him to bear, for He holds up worlds, He rules over all the affairs of the universe. Nothing that in any way concerns our peace is too small for Him to notice... 'He healeth the broken in heart, and bindeth up their wounds.' Psalm 147:3. The relations between God and each soul are as distinct and full as though there were not another soul upon the earth to share His watchcare, not another soul for whom He gave His beloved Son." Also, on p. 68, Sister White goes on to say, "By calm, simple faith, the soul holds communion with God, and gathers to itself rays of light to strengthen and sustain it in the conflict with Satan. God is our tower of divine strength."

I recently had a dream, and in my dream, a few of us were at a hospital singing to the patients. In one particular room, the nurses asked us to go sing to that patient who was dying and needed power to get well. She was needing prayer for healing, and so after we had sung the song to her, "I Sing the Mighty Power of God," and then we had a prayer for her, and when prayer had been offered for her, the word "POWER" lighted up and flashed and showed up on her computer screen on her life support machine, keeping her alive, that she was hooked up to. The two nurses and all of us in the room saw the word, "POWER" on the screen, and we all saw and felt the power of God and knew that God was hearing the sincere prayer of faith offered for this patient! The nurses thanked us for coming! It felt so good to be used of God to be a help and a blessing to others and to make a difference in someone's life! That's what life is all about like Isaiah 58 says.

End of Dream.

I remember hearing of an experiment that was made on patients in the ICU in the hospital. They found that the patients being prayed for did better than the patients not prayed for. There's Power in Prayer! (Read

Sister White's book *Ministry of Healing*). We saw the power of prayer, when we prayed for Jonathan the times he was in the hospital!

In Luke 22:31 and 32 we read, "And the Lord said, Simon, Simon, (or you can put your name in there—Jonathan, Jonathan) behold, Satan hath desired to have you, that he may sift you as wheat: But I have prayed for thee, that thy faith fail not: and when thou art converted, strengthen thy brethren." These are the words of Jesus spoken in red in the Bible. We, too, are praying earnestly for Jonathan!

Read in *Steps to Christ* by E.G. White, the chapter "Growing Up Into Christ" pp. 45–51, especially p. 49. "Rest in God. He is able to keep that which you have committed to Him. If you will leave yourself in His hands, He will bring you off more than conqueror through Him that has loved you... But let us keep our eyes fixed upon Christ, and He will preserve us. Looking unto Jesus, we are safe. Nothing can pluck us out of His hand. In constantly beholding Him, we are changed into the same image from glory to glory, even as by the Spirit of the Lord.' 2 Corinthians 3:18. It was thus that the early disciples gained their likeness to the dear Saviour. When those disciples heard the words of Jesus, they felt their need of Him. They sought, they found, they followed Him. They were with Him in the house, at the table, in the closet, in the field. They were with Him as pupils with a teacher daily receiving from His lips lessons of holy truth. They looked to Him, as servants to their master, to learn their duty. Those disciples were men 'subject to like passions as we are'. James 5:17. They had the same battle with sin to fight. They needed the same grace, in order to live a holy life." So do we need Jesus to help us.

One time while Jonathan was sleeping in his chair, where he'd been watching sermons, he spoke up in his sleep and said, "I couldn't live without you!" I figured he was talking to Jesus in his sleep. But, I spoke up and said to him, "I couldn't live without you either, Jonathan. We all need Jesus and we all need one another." We're so thankful Jesus is keeping Jonathan safe on the "Ark" and not falling apart spiritually and physically in some old nursing home and dying lost! Thank you Jesus! Praise the Lord! We keep praying for his salvation and that he'll soon respond to the Holy Spirit and surrender <u>all</u> to Jesus and give up these drugs he's on! It's all in God's hands!

Read in *Steps to Christ* by E.G. White, pp. 58, 59, 65 in the two chapters, "A Knowledge of God" and "The Privilege of Prayer": "Many are the ways in which God is seeking to make Himself known to us and bring us into communion with Him. Nature speaks to our senses without ceasing. The open heart will be impressed with the love and glory of God as revealed through the works of His hands... If we will but listen, God's created works will teach us precious lessons of obedience and trust... And God cares for everything and sustains everything that He has created. He who upholds the unnumbered worlds throughout immensity, at the same time cares for the wants of the little brown sparrow that sings its humble song without fear... No tears are shed that God does not notice. There is no smile that He does not mark. If we would fully believe this, all undue anxieties would be dismissed. Our lives would not be so filled with disappointment as now; for everything, whether great or small, would be left in the hands of God, who is not perplexed by the multiplicity of cares, or overwhelmed by their weight. We should then enjoy a rest of soul to which many have long been strangers... What can the angels of heaven think of poor helpless human being, who are subject to temptation, when God's heart of infinite love yearns toward them, ready to give them more than they can ask or think, and yet they pray so little, and have so little faith?... The darkness of the evil one encloses those who neglect to pray. The whispered temptations of the enemy entice them to sin; and it is all because they do not make use of the privileges that God has given them in the divine appointment of prayer. Why should the sons and daughters of God be reluctant to pray, when prayer is the key in the hand of faith to unlock heaven's storehouse, where are treasured the boundless resources of Omnipotence? Without unceasing prayer and diligent watching we are in danger of growing careless and of deviating from the right path. The adversary seeks continually to obstruct the way to the mercy-seat, that we may not by earnest supplication and faith obtain grace and power to resist temptation."

We hope to soon be able to end this story of Jonathan's journey with the words, "Jonathan has surrendered all to Jesus and wants to live and please Jesus and not himself." We continue to pray in faith for this experience to happen! Praise God! God is in control with His unseen hands!

On p. 29 in *Last Day Events* by E. G. White, we read, "The world is not without a ruler. The program of coming events is in the hands of the Lord. The Majesty of heaven has the destiny of nations as well as the concerns of His church in His own charge... In the great closing work we shall meet with perplexities that we know not how to deal with, but let us not forget that the three great Powers of heaven are working, that a divine hand is on the wheel, and that God will bring His purposes to pass.

As the wheel-like complications were under the guidance of the hand beneath the wings of the cherubim, so the complicated play of human events is under divine control. Amidst the strife and tumult of nations, He that sitteth above the cherubim still guides the affairs of the earth... (See Ezekiel 1:4, 26; 10:8; Daniel 4:17, 25, 32). Read in *Ministry of Healing* by E. G. White on pp. 158–159, "Those who are fighting the battle of life at great odds may be strengthened and encouraged by little attentions that cost only a loving effort. To such the strong, helpful grasp of the hand by a true friend is worth more than gold or silver. Words of kindness are as welcome as the smile of angels... Heavenly intelligences are waiting to co-operate with human instrumentalities, that they may reveal to the world what human beings may become, and what, through union with the Divine, may be accomplished for the saving of souls that are ready to perish. There is no limit to the usefulness of one who, putting self aside, makes room for the working of the Holy Spirit upon his heart and lives a life wholly consecrated to God. All who consecrate body, soul, and spirit to His service will be constantly receiving a new endowment of physical, mental, and spiritual power. The inexhaustible supplies of heaven are at their command. Christ gives them the breath of His own Spirit, the life of His own life. The Holy Spirit puts forth its highest energies to work in mind and heart...".

Continue reading on p. 160, "To everyone who offers himself to the Lord for service, withholding nothing, is given power for the attainment of measureless results. For these God will do great things." Read in *Ministry of Healing* by E. G. White the chapters: "Teaching and Healing"; "Helping the Tempted"; "Working for the Intemperate". Continue to read on pp. 181–182, "Talk courage to the people; lift them up to God in prayer... Nothing is apparently more helpless, yet really more invincible, than the soul that feels its nothingness and relies wholly on the merits of the Saviour. By prayer, by the study of His word, by faith in His abiding presence, the weakest of human beings may live in contact with the living Christ, and He will hold them by a hand that will never let go.

These precious words every soul that abides in Christ may make his own. He may say: Micah 7:7, 8, 19; Isaiah 13:12; Psalm 68:13. Those whom Christ has forgiven most will love Him most. Those are they who in the final day will stand nearest to His throne. 'They shall see His face; and His name shall be in their foreheads.' Revelation 22:4." Also, read Philippians 4:13, 19. Also, read in *Ministry of Healing* pp. 178–180, "All who give evidence of true conversion should be encouraged to work for others. Let none turn away a soul who leaves the service of Satan for the service of Christ. When one gives evidence that the Spirit of God is striving with him, present every encouragement for entering the Lord's service. 'Of some have compassion, making a difference.' Jude 22... When light flashes into the soul, some who appeared to be most fully given to sin will become successful workers for just such sinners as they themselves once were... These can help others. The one who has been tempted and tried, whose hope was well-nigh gone, but who was saved by hearing a message of love, can understand the science of soul-saving. He whose heart is filled with love for Christ because he himself has been sought for by the Saviour and brought back to the fold, knows how to seek the lost. He can point sinners to the Lamb of God. He has given himself without reserve to God and has been accepted in the Beloved. The hand that in weakness was held out for help has been grasped. By the ministry of such ones many prodigals will be brought to the Father.

For every soul struggling to rise from a life of sin to a life of purity, the great element of power abides in the only 'name under heaven given among men, whereby we must be saved.'" Acts 4:12. 'If any man thirst' for restful hope, for deliverance from sinful propensities, Christ says, 'let him come unto Me, and drink.' John 7:37. The only remedy for vice is the grace and power of Christ... True reformation begins with soul cleansing... Only those who honor Him can He honor. Man's conduct in this world decides his eternal destiny. As he has sown, so he must reap. Cause will be followed by effect."

Read also on pp. 171–178, "Earnest effort should be made in behalf of those who are in bondage to evil habits... Health and character are ruined... The hearts of the parents are broken. Men speak of these erring ones as hopeless; but not so does God regard them. He understands all the circumstances that have made them what they are, and He looks upon them with pity. This is a class that demand help... Among the victims of intemperance are men of all classes and all professions... Some of them who were once in the possession of wealth are without home, without friends, in suffering, misery, disease, and degradation. They have lost their self-control. Unless a helping hand is held out to them, they will sink lower and lower. With these, self-indulgence is not only a moral sin, but a physical disease. Often in helping the intemperate we must, as Christ so often did, give first attention to their physical condition. They need wholesome, unstimulating food and drink, clean clothing, opportunity to secure physical cleanliness. They need to be surrounded with an atmosphere of helpful, uplifting Christian influence... In dealing with the victims of intemperance we must remember that we are not dealing with sane men, but with those who for the time being are under the power of a demon. Be patient and forbearing. Think not of the repulsive, forbidding appearance, but of the precious life that Christ died to redeem... Speak no word of censure... Help him to rise. Speak words that will encourage faith. Seek to strengthen every good trait in his character. Teach him how to reach upward... Help him to see the value of the talents which God has given him, but which he has neglected to improve.

"Although the will has been depraved and weakened, there is hope for him in Christ... Open the Bible before the tempted, struggling one, and over and over again read to him the promises of God. These promises will be to him as the leaves of the tree of life... You must hold fast to those whom you are trying to help, else victory will never be yours...

"They have decided to make an effort to live for Christ; but their will power is weakened, and they must be carefully guarded by those who watch for souls as they that must give an account... Many have to battle against strong hereditary tendencies to evil. Unnatural cravings, sensual impulses, were their inheritance from birth. These must be carefully guarded against. Within and without, good and evil are striving for the mastery. Those who have never passed through such experiences cannot know the almost overmastering power of appetite or the fierceness of the conflict between habits of self-indulgence and the determination to be temperate in all things. Over and over again the battle must be fought... Remember that you do not work alone. Ministering angels unite in service with every truehearted son and daughter of God. And Christ is the restorer. The Great Physician Himself stands beside His faithful workers, saying to the repentant soul, "Child, thy sins be forgiven thee." Mark 2:5... The victims of evil habit must be aroused to the necessity of making an effort for themselves. Others may put forth the most earnest endeavor to uplift them, the grace of God may be freely offered, Christ may entreat, His angels may minister; but all will be in vain unless they themselves are roused to fight the battle in their own behalf... Feeling the terrible power of temptation, the drawing of desire that leads to indulgence, many a man cries in despair, "I cannot resist evil." Tell him that he can, that he must resist. (Read Jude 24; Philippians 4:13; James 4:7–10). He may have been overcome again and again, but it need not be always thus. He is weak in moral power, controlled by the habits of a life of sin. His promises and resolutions are like ropes of sand. The knowledge of his broken promises and forfeited pledges weakens his confidence in his own sincerity and causes him to feel that God cannot accept him or work with his efforts. But he need not despair.

"Those who put their trust in Christ are not to be enslaved by any hereditary or cultivated habit or tendency. Instead of being held in bondage to the lower nature, they are to rule every appetite and passion.

God has not left us to battle with evil in our own finite strength. Whatever may be our inherited or cultivated tendencies to wrong, we can overcome through the power that He is ready to impart. The tempted one needs to understand the true force of the will. This is the governing power in the nature of man—the power of decision, of choice. Everything depends on the right action of the will. Desires for goodness and purity are right, so far as they go; but if we stop here, they avail nothing. Many will go down to ruin while hoping and desiring to overcome their evil propensities. They do not yield the will to God. They do not <u>choose</u> to serve Him. God has given us the power of choice; it is ours to exercise. We cannot change our hearts, we cannot control our thoughts, our impulses, our affections. We cannot make ourselves pure, fit for God's service. But we can <u>choose</u> to serve God, we can give Him our will; then He will work in us to will and to do according to His good pleasure. Thus, our whole nature will be brought under the control of Christ. Through the right exercise of the will, an entire change may be made in the life. By yielding up the will to Christ, we ally ourselves with divine power. We receive strength from above to hold us steadfast. A pure and noble life, a life of victory over appetite and lust, is possible to everyone who will unite his weak, wavering human will to the omnipotent, unwavering will of God. Those who are struggling against the power of appetite should be instructed in the principles of healthful living. They should be shown that violation of the laws of health, by creating diseased conditions and unnatural cravings, lays the foundation of the liquor habit. Only by living in obedience to the principles of health can they hope to be freed from the craving for unnatural stimulants. While they depend upon divine strength to break the bonds of appetite, they are to co-operate with God by obedience to His laws, both moral and physical. Those who are endeavoring to reform should be provided with employment. None who are able to labor should be taught to expect food and clothing and shelter free of cost. For their own sake, as well as for the sake of others, some way should be devised whereby they may return an equivalent for what they receive. Encourage every effort toward self-support. This will strengthen self-respect and a noble independence. And occupation of mind and body in useful work is essential as a safeguard against temptation… Only in distrust of self and dependence on the mercy of Christ can they stand. All who give evidence of true conversion should be encouraged to work for others."

In the book, *My Life Today* by E. G. White, she writes on p. 305, "Human agencies are the hands of heavenly instrumentalities, for heavenly angels employ human hands in practical ministry… The knowledge and actions of the heavenly order of workers, united with the knowledge and power which are imparted to human agencies, relieve the oppressed and distressed. The very angels who when Satan was seeking the supremacy fought the battle in the heavenly courts and triumphed on the side of God; the very angels who from their exalted position shouted for joy over the creation of our world and over the creation of our first parents who were to inhabit the earth… are most intensely interested to work in union with the fallen, redeemed race in the development of that power which God gives to help every man who will unite with heavenly intelligences to seek and save human beings who are perishing in their sins." Sister White writes in her book *Thoughts From the Mount of Blessings* on pp. 116–119, "'Bring us not into temptation, but deliver us from the evil one.'—Matthew 6:13, R.V. Temptation is enticement to sin, and this does not proceed from God, but from Satan and from the evil of our own hearts… Satan seeks to bring us into temptation, that the evil of our characters may be revealed before men and angels, that he may claim us as his own… The enemy leads us into sin, and then he accuses us before the heavenly universe as unworthy of the love of God. But "the Lord said unto Satan, The Lord rebuke thee, O Satan; even the Lord that hath chosen Jerusalem rebuke thee: is not this a brand plucked out of the fire?" And unto Joshua He said, "Behold, I have caused thine iniquity to pass from thee, and I will clothe thee with change of raiment." Zechariah 3:1–4. God in His great love is seeking to develop in us the precious graces of His Spirit. He permits us to encounter obstacles, persecution, and hardships, not as a curse, but as the greatest blessing of our lives. Every temptation resisted, every trial bravely borne, gives us a new experience and advances us in the work of character building. The soul that through divine power resists temptation reveals to the world and to the heavenly universe the efficiency of the grace of Christ. But while we are not to be dismayed by trial, bitter though it be, we should pray that God will not permit us to be brought where we shall be drawn away by the desires of our own evil hearts… We shall wait for His hand to lead us; we shall listen to His voice, saying, "This is the way, walk ye in it." Isaiah 30:21. It is not safe for us to linger to contemplate the advantages to be reaped through yielding to Satan's suggestions. Sin means dishonor and disaster to every soul that indulges in it; but it is blinding and deceiving in its nature, and it will entice us with flattering presentations. If we venture on Satan's ground we have no assurance of protection from his power. So far as in us lies, we should close every avenue by which the tempter may find access to us. The prayer, "Bring us not into temptation," is itself a promise. If we commit ourselves to God we have the assurance,

He "will not suffer you to be tempted above that ye are able; but will with the temptation also make a way to escape, that ye may be able to bear it." 1 Corinthians 10:13.

"The only safeguard against evil is the indwelling of Christ in the heart through faith in His righteousness. It is because selfishness exists in our hearts that temptation has power over us. But when we behold the great love of God, selfishness appears to us in its hideous and repulsive character, and we desire to have it expelled from the soul. As the Holy Spirit glorifies Christ, our hearts are softened and subdued, the temptation loses its power, and the grace of Christ transforms the character. Christ will never abandon the soul for whom He has died. The soul may leave Him and be overwhelmed with temptation, but Christ can never turn from one for whom He has paid the ransom of His own life. Could our spiritual vision be quickened, we should see souls bowed under oppression and burdened with grief, pressed as a cart beneath sheaves and ready to die in discouragement. We should see angels flying swiftly to aid these tempted ones, who are standing as on the brink of a precipice. The angels from heaven force back the hosts of evil that encompass these souls, and guide them to plant their feet on the sure foundation. The battles waging between the two armies are as real as those fought by the armies of this world, and on the issue of the spiritual conflict eternal destinies depend. To us, as to Peter, the word is spoken, "Satan hath desired to have you, that he may sift you as wheat: but I have prayed for thee, that thy faith fail not." Luke 22:31, 32. Thank God, we are not left alone. He who "so loved the world, that He gave His only-begotten Son, that whosoever believeth in Him should not perish, but have everlasting life" (John 3:16), will not desert us in the battle with the adversary of God and man. "Behold," He says, "I give unto you power to tread on serpents and scorpions, and over all the power of the enemy: and nothing shall by any means hurt you." Luke 10:19. Live in contact with the living Christ, and He will hold you firmly by a hand that will never let go. Know and believe the love that God has to us, and you are secure; that love is a fortress impregnable to all the delusions and assaults of Satan. "The name of the Lord is a strong tower: the righteous runneth into it, and is safe." Proverbs 18:10." Read also, Psalm 31:14, 15; Psalm 34; Psalm 37:23–40; Psalm 38:15, 21, 22.

God is still in control of things going on in Jonathan's life and He can overrule Satan and his plans to destroy Jonathan. We pray that soon Jonathan will yield to the Holy Spirit's power and turn from his life of sin to follow Jesus with all his heart, soul, mind and spirit. And take up his cross daily like Luke 9:23 says, "And He said to them all, if any man will come after me, let him deny himself, and take up his cross daily, and follow me." (Continue to read verses 24–27, too). Read Luke 10:25–37. In Isaiah 9:17 God says, "For all this his anger is not turned away, but his hand is stretched out still."

One time Jonathan was sleeping in his easy chair and he was repeating Psalm 23 in his sleep out loud. When I walked passed him sleeping in his easy chair, I could hear him repeating verse 4 in his sleep, "Yea, though I walk through the valley of the shadow of death, I will fear no evil: for thou art with me; thy rod and thy staff they comfort me." When he woke up he said to me, "I was dreaming Psalm 23 and repeating it." I said, "Yes, I heard you in your sleep repeating it."

Another time Jonathan was taking a nap in his easy chair in the front room and in his sleep he said, "MOM! Help me find my Robe! Hurry up!" I said to him, "You mean your Robe of Christ's Righteousness?" I then prayed, "Lord please help Jonathan find his Robe of Christ's Righteousness and put it on before it's too late! Thank you Jesus! Amen."

There was a time when Jonathan was admitted to the hospital because he was depressed. I sent him some materials and a letter to try to encourage him. The following is a copy of the materials I sent him and the letter I wrote him:

March 23, 2017, Matthew 11:28–30

"Our dear son, Jonathan, Get well soon! We love you and miss you and Mom and Dad love you and we're praying for you!!!

Remember, Jesus loves you and Jesus is stronger than Satan! Jude 24, Philippians 4:13

Cling to Jesus and not your sins! Matthew 11:28-30, John 3:16.

Have faith in God to help heal you! Matthew 21:22.

Take care of yourself and hurry home!

Hugs and kisses! Love, Mom and Dad xo

"I Refuse to be Discouraged!"

I refuse to be discouraged,

To be sad, or to cry;

I refuse to be downhearted,

And here's the reason why.

I have a God who's mighty

Who's sovereign and supreme;
I have a God who loves me,
And I am on His team.
He is all-wise and powerful,
Jesus is His name;
Though everything is changeable,
My God remains the same.
My God knows all that's happening,
Beginning to the end;
His presence is my comfort,
He is my dearest Friend.
When sickness comes to weaken me,
To bring my head down low;
I call upon my mighty God,
Into His arms I go.
When circumstances threaten,
To rob me of my peace;
He draws me close unto His breast,
Where all my strivings cease.
When my heart melts within me,
And weakness takes control;
He gathers me into His arms,
He soothes my heart and soul.
The great "I AM" is with me,
My life is in His hand;
The "Son of God" He is my hope,
It's in His strength I stand.
I refuse to be defeated,
My eyes are on my God;
He has promised to be with me,

As through this life I trod.

I'm looking past all circumstances,

To Heaven's throne above;

My prayers have reached the heart of God,

I'm resting in His love.

I give God thanks in everything,

My eyes are on His face;

The battle's His, the vict'ry mine,

He'll help me win the race!

(author unknown)

I can do all things through Christ

who strengthens me!

Philippians 4:13

"A Prayer for Today"

This is the beginning of a new day. God has given me this day to use as I will. I can waste it – or use it for good, but what I do today is important, because I am exchanging a day of my life for it! When tomorrow comes, this day will be gone forever; leaving in its place something that I have traded for it. I want it to be gain, and not loss; good, and not evil; success, and not failure; in order that I shall not regret the price that I have paid for it."

Dr. Heartsill Wilson

"Peace to You!"

"'If Thou canst do anything, have compassion on us, and help us.' How many a sin-burdened soul has echoed that prayer. And to all, the pitying Saviour's answer is, 'If thou canst believe, all things are possible to him that believeth.' It is faith that connects us with heaven, and brings us strength for coping with the powers of darkness. In Christ, God has provided means for subduing <u>every</u> sinful trait, and resisting <u>every</u> temptation, however strong. But many feel that they lack faith, and therefore they remain away from Christ. Let these souls, in their helpless unworthiness, cast themselves upon the mercy of their compassionate Saviour. Look not to self, but to Christ. He who healed the sick and cast out demons when He walked among men is the same mighty Redeemer today. Faith comes by the word of God. Then grasp His promise, 'Him that cometh to Me I will in no wise cast out.' John 6:37. Cast yourself at His feet with the cry, 'Lord, I believe; help *Thou* mine unbelief.' You can never perish while you do this—never." *Desire of Ages*, p. 429. Praise God, friend. Praise God!

"THE GOOSE STORY"

Next fall when you see geese heading south for the winter.... flying along in the V-formation.... you might consider what science has discovered as to why they fly that way. As each bird flaps its wings, it creates uplift for the bird immediately following.

By flying in the V-formation the whole flock adds at least 71% greater flying range than if each bird flew on its own.

People who share a common direction and sense of community can get where they are going more quickly and easily because they are traveling on the thrust of one another.

When a goose falls out of formation, it suddenly feels the drag and resistance of trying to go it alone... and quickly gets back into formation to take advantage of the lifting power of the bird in front.

If we have the sense of a goose, we will stand by each other like that

If we have as much sense as a goose, we will stay in formation with those who are headed the same way we are. When the head goose gets tired, it rotates back in the wing and another goose flies point.

It is sensible to take turns doing demanding jobs with people or with geese flying south.

Geese honk from behind to encourage those up front to keep up their speed. What do we say when we honk from behind?

Finally, and this is important.... When a goose gets sick, or is wounded by gunshots and falls out of formation, two other geese fall out with that goose and follow it down to lend help and protection. They stay with the fallen goose until it is able to fly or until it dies: only then do they launch out on their own or with another formation to catch up with their group.

If we have the sense of a goose, we will stand by each other like that.

I Would Be Like Jesus

*Seek those things which are above, where Christ sitteth on the right hand of God....
For ye are dead, and your life is hid with Christ in God. Col. 3:1-3; Php. 1:21 As he is, so are we in this world. 1 Jn. 4:17*

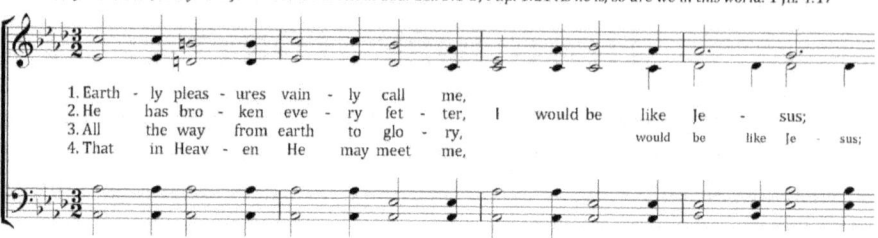

1. Earth-ly pleas-ures vain-ly call me,
2. He has bro-ken eve-ry fet-ter,
3. All the way from earth to glo-ry,
4. That in Heav-en He may meet me,

I would be like Je-sus; would be like Je-sus;

Noth-ing world-ly shall en-thrall me,
That my soul may serve Him bet-ter,
Tell-ing o'er and o'er the sto-ry,
That His words "Well done" may greet me,

I would be like Je-sus. would be like Je-sus.

Refrain

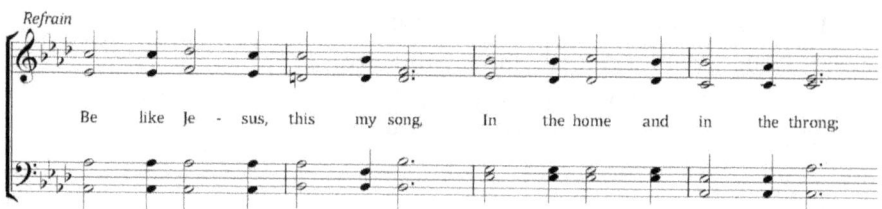

Be like Je-sus, this my song, In the home and in the throng;

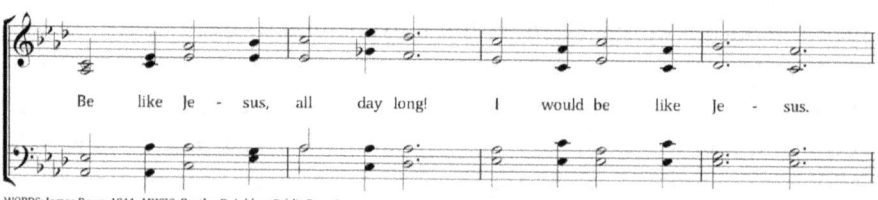

Be like Je-sus, all day long! I would be like Je-sus.

WORDS: James Rowe, 1911. MUSIC: Bentley D. Ackley. Public Domain.

"NOW—Don't Put It Off!"
Written by Linda Clore, June 7, 2017

Don't put it off, what you can do today,
So you can make your life a better way!
For no one knows what tomorrow may hold!
Obey Jesus and do as you are told!
Make your choice to put your life in God's Hand!
And remain true to Him and take your stand!
This old world is soon to come to an end!
<u>NOW</u> is the time for you to part with sin!
And surrender your <u>all</u> to Jesus Christ,
And be determined to end all your strife!
And choose to be at peace with God and man!
Choose to enter into that better land!
It's there where <u>all</u> our trials we will lay down!
And there receive our robe and harp and crown!
The decisions we're making day by day,
Determines how our journey ends some day!
So, don't put it off, give Jesus your heart!
And with Gods' help, <u>now</u>, with your sins depart!
We're living in serious and solemn times!
Lives are hanging in the balance all the time!
How we're living <u>now</u> decides our destiny!
<u>Now's</u> the time for you to gain the victory!
Be ready to look in Christ's face without fear!
Because we know His coming is drawing near!
So, don't put it off! Get rid of your sins <u>now</u>!
And enjoy the smiles of God, and not His frown!
Jesus left all heaven and died to save you!
Won't you prove your love to Jesus and be true?!
All you have is <u>NOW</u>! Tomorrow may be too late!
Don't put it off! Decide <u>NOW</u> what will be your fate!
Surrender <u>all</u> to Jesus without delay!
And be ready and prepared for 'Judgment Day'!
Be ready to look in Christ's face without fear!

Because we know His coming is drawing near!
There's no one that can make this decision for you!
NOW is all you have! What are you going to do?!

Read "Thoughts from the Mount of Blessing" by E.G. White pp. 116-119 on Matthew 6:13

Christian Television | Radio | Music

Counteracting the counterfeit by proclaiming the three angels' messages of Revelation 14 to the world.

August 10, 2017

David & Linda Clore
2645 Arkansas Terrace
Quenemo, KS 66528

Dear Clore Family,

I always appreciate hearing from you, and learning what the Lord is doing in your lives! Thank you for keeping me updated on the doors God is opening for you all. Praise God that He can forgive and cleanse us, and empower us to live a life of victory. You're right, He wants to transform us into His image, so we will be like Him when He comes again soon. That's why 3ABN exists, as well, to proclaim this undiluted gospel message to a lost and dying world! Thank you for joining hands with us in helping to spread this message.

Know that your 3ABN Family will be praying for you, as you seek to raise funds for publishing your next book through Teach Services. I also so appreciate your prayers for 3ABN and my brother, Kenny, as he recovers after his heart surgery. Our God is faithful to hear and answer!

May God continue to bless your ministry for Him there in Kansas. Remain faithful to Him, and soon we'll hear those words, "Well done, My good and faithful servant."

His Love and Ours,

Danny Shelton
President & CEO

DS:jm

3ABN.tv

Danny Shelton | President | CEO
danny.shelton@3abn.org

P.O. Box 220 | West Frankfort, IL 62896 | phone 618-627-4651 | fax 618-627-2726

"Experiences" written by Linda Clore, May 31, 2017

That morning on May 29, 2017 when we got up, we noticed it was looking terribly stormy, so we turned on the radio weather station and it said, "In the forecast for today, there's tornadoes with hail the size of baseballs and 70 mph damaging winds with heavy rains."

We knew the devil delights in destruction and to steal and kill as John 10:10 says. We were having our morning worship and praying for God's protection over us and the "Ark" in these dangerous storms forecasted. As we continued to have our worship, the clouds grew heavy and it began to thunder and grow darker and darker! We could see the angry clouds forming and we kept praying God would please let the storm pass by us and protect us and our house trailer and windows and car and garden and fruit on our fruit trees! I remarked about them forecasting hail the size of baseballs and how in Revelation 16 it described the 7 last plagues and in verse 21 it said, "And there fell upon men a great hail out of heaven, every stone about the weight of a talent; and men blasphemed God because of the plague of the hail; for the plague thereof was exceeding great." (Some scholars have estimated a talent to be 66 pounds in weight or more.)

I prayed God would please put His protective right hand over us, like I had seen one time in a cloud formation over our place, an enormous gigantic cloud in the form of a right hand covering over the "Ark". I prayed also that God would please send His Angel's wings drawn over us and protect us, like I had seen one time in a cloud formation covering over our place, an angel with his wings spread out and covering over our whole "Ark"!

Read in *Early Writings* by E. G. White, "The Open and Shut Door" on pp. 42-45. On p. 43 she writes, "Satan is now using every device in this sealing time to keep the minds of God's people from the present truth and to cause them to waver. I saw a covering that God was drawing over His people to protect them in the time of trouble; and every soul that was decided on the truth and was pure in heart was to be covered with the covering of the Almighty..." On p. 44 she continues to say, "Satan was trying his every art to hold them where they were, until the sealing was past, until the covering was drawn over God's people, and they left without a shelter from the burning wrath of God, in the seven last plagues. God has begun to draw this covering over His people, and it will soon be drawn over all who are to have a shelter in the day of slaughter. God will work in power for His people; and Satan will be permitted to work also."

As we continued to have our worship, we could see the dark angry clouds pass by and the storm passed and the sun came out! Praise the Lord! Thank you Jesus! We prayed and thank the good Lord for protecting us from the fierce storm that had just passed by and we didn't lose our electricity either! God is so good!

Then, the next day on May 30, 2017, we were having our evening worship and as we were praying and studying God's Word, it grew really dark and threatening clouds, black and heavy, and the wind came up strong and we heard the thunder rolling! Again, we prayed for God's protection over us and the "Ark". Then, it passed on by us with no dangerous or damaging storm hitting us on the "Ark". Praise the Lord! We, again, prayed and thanked the good Lord for sparing us again from what could have been a disaster!

Then, David spoke up and said, "Turn the radio weather station on and see what they were saying." They were saying, "A severe storm warning threat for East Osage County was cancelled, and the storm was no longer a threat! Also, the severe storm threat for N.W. Franklin County had moved out of the area and was no longer a threat of damaging tornadoes! This was the exact spot where we were at! We prayed again and thanked the good Lord for hearing our earnest prayers again for His loving protective care over us and the "Ark" and for taking care of us from these terrible damaging storms that He let pass by us with no damage done to us or our place! We just praised the Lord for His covering placed over us and the "Ark" we're preparing for God's people to come to for protection during the Sunday Law crises, when we won't be able to buy or sell and we'll need this "Ark", God has helped us to build and has protected over and over again from Satan trying to destroy us and our place of refuge to go through the time of trouble soon to be upon us! Now's the time to prepare spiritually and physically for the storms ahead of us, when every earthly support will be cut off to those who stay true and loyal to God's 7th day Sabbath and all His 10 Commandments, as *Desire of Ages* by E. G. White, pp. 121-122 says.

Again, on May 31, 2017, another storm was forecast on the radio weather station with possible tornadoes, hail, damaging winds and heavy rains! Again, we had our morning worship and again prayed for God's protection over us in the dangerous storms forecast! The terribly dangerous dark black clouds formed over us and it began to thunder and rain! We prayed God would please give us a much needed rain, but no bad storms or tornadoes! Again, God heard our sincere prayers for protection over us and the "Ark" and for rain! Thank you Jesus! Praise the

Lord! God is so good to look out for us and the "Ark". We didn't lose our electricity either. The radio weather station said we'll have these terrible storms all week. We pray God will spare us from any dangerous storm blowing around out there! We serve a Great and wonderful and mighty God! We love you, Lord!

Episode #1:

Another experience we had was, we were air-popping our popcorn to eat for breakfast. I had been praying and asking God to please, <u>TODAY</u>, convert Jonathan! Then, as I was eating my popcorn, a kernel of popcorn stuck on my finger, and it looked like a "?" (question mark). I know God won't force us to serve and obey Him! God gives us the power of choice to make our decision to follow and obey Him or not. (I had dad take a picture of the piece of popcorn looking like a question mark). It's up to Jonathan, and each one of us, when we'll decide to surrender <u>all</u> to Jesus! Jesus loves us and woos us to Him. God, dad and I want Jonathan "<u>TODAY</u>" to love and obey and follow Jesus, and go <u>all</u> the way with Jesus <u>NOW</u>, and see how much happier and healthier he'll be serving the Lord with <u>all</u> his heart and going <u>all</u> the way with the Lord! But we know God won't force His will on any of us. We know it has to be Jonathan's decision when that choice and decision will be made! We just keep praying for him!

Psalm 95:7, 8, we claim for Jonathan. He's wanting to go back into a nursing home and not stay here with us because we're taking his nicotine and coffee pills away. Jonathan feels too that we're too old to care for him. Read in *Ministry of Healing* the chapter "The Co-Working of the Divine and the Human" by E. G. White, pp. 111-124.

Jonathan became depressed and wanted to be taken to the Emergency room and be admitted to the hospital for his depression, and from there be taken to a nursing home facility to be cared for and not come back home. We had prayer with him and tried to encourage him to stay home with us and improve his health, getting off his nicotine and coffee pills. He had had a blood pressure of 210/110 and we were afraid he'd have a stroke or a heart attack! The doctor had had to put him on a second blood pressure medicine to try and bring it down. But he still wanted to leave and be put in a nursing home where he could take what he wanted and do what he wanted.

So, I got his things together. The weather station radio was saying severe storms and hail and strong winds and possible tornadoes. But Jonathan still wanted to be taken to the Emergency room and admitted for his depression in a hospital.

We prayed with Jonathan that he would change his mind and that he'd get well and want to come on home. As dad and Jonathan drove off to Ottawa, it began to sprinkle. By the time dad and Jonathan had reached Ottawa, there had been a terrible storm go through Ottawa before they got there! At the emergency room entrance, dad saw two ladies sitting outside on the bench and he said, "What has happened in this city with all the debris all over the streets and everywhere?"

They both started telling him of the terrible storm that just passed through with golf ball size hail and strong winds and tons of rain smashing windows in houses and cars and denting in cars and causing terrible damage all over town! Dad gave each of them a 3ABN sharing card and said, "That is so terrible about the storm!"

Both the ladies were so happy to get the 3ABN sharing card telling of all the different programs they offer and thanked David for sharing the cards with them.

Jonathan was seen in the Emergency room and admitted to a rehabilitating center to help his depression. Dad then began his journey home. It just poured and poured and he had to drive 30 mph because he couldn't see! Praise God! The Lord got him safely home through the storm! There was no damage here! We thanked the good Lord for His protective care over us and our place. God heard our prayers. We continue to pray for Jonathan's healing and protection, and his conversion! Jonathan is in God's hands! We pray God will be in control of Jonathan and his life. It's so sad to have him leave home. We have no idea what will be in Jonathan's future at this time! All we can do is pray that God will help him through this crisis he's going through and hold him in God's unseen hand. Jonathan's Journey is an ongoing journey that will take probably another book to write. Please pray for him for time is running out for all of us! In each of our journeys of life, there's a record being kept on each one of us that we will have to meet some day soon! The decision we're making day by day will determine how our journey will someday end. Let's put Christ first in our life! Matthew 6:33. Read *Great Controversy* by E. G. White, chapter 28 "Facing Our Life's Record" (The Investigative Judgment) pp. 479-491.

Jonathan may be out of our hands—but he's still in God's unseen hand! And he may be out of our sight—but he's not out of our heart! He's still in God's sight, watching over him. He's still in our prayers and he still has our love and God's love! Joshua 1:9 "Have not I commanded thee? Be strong and of a good courage; be not afraid, neither be thou dismayed: for the Lord thy God is with thee whithersoever thou goest."

Jonathan, like the prodigal son in Luke 15, has gone off to a far country to do as he pleases. He's in Kansas City, Missouri in a hospital for his depression. Like the father of the prodigal, we earnestly pray for Jonathan to come to his senses and be converted and come home and change his ways! It's all in God's unseen hand!

Just recently I dreamed Sister White's quote found in *Review & Herald* 3/9/1905, "Strive to be among the 144,000." And on p. 211 in *Last Day Events* by E. G. White, "Many who have strayed from the fold will come back to follow the great Shepherd." Read also pp. 268–269.

I believe Jonathan will return back to Jesus before He comes! This is my earnest prayer for our son, Jonathan! Praise God! Thank you Jesus!

Read: *Counsels on Diet and Foods* by E. G. White, pp. 28–40; 57–64, 353–355, 380–384.

Also read, *Maranatha* by E. G. White, p. 108; *Last Day Events* by E. G. White, p. 74; *5T* by E. G. White, pp 132–148, 191–202; *7T* by E. G. White pp. 42–44.

Jonathan did return back home from his stay in the hospital for his depression. He still keeps wanting to stay on his doctor's drugs and stay on his nicotine. He still keeps having depression and panic attacks. He says he loves the Lord and wants to go to heaven. I say to him that he needs to put Christ first in his life and give up the things he knows to be wrong and let Jesus take full control of his life and let God clear up his mind and surrender all to Jesus, and find peace and joy and happiness in the Lord, and healing.

We continue to pray for our son, Jonathan, that he'll wake up out of his stupor and see what God can do for him.

Read Episode Two: Experiences Jonathan went through and God watched over him. Please keep praying for him! Thanks! And us, too. Thanks!

I may have to prepare another episode of "Jonathan's Journey" telling of his walk with God and how God's unseen hand finally rescued him from the devil's hold on him. "For with God nothing shall be impossible." Luke 1:37.

Episode # 2:

"Jonathan's Journey"
Some experiences Jonathan has gone through:
Panic Attack!
What Do People See in You?
The Seizure!
"PANIC ATTACK!"

Written by Linda Clore, October 29, 2015

I would like to close my book with this final story I've entitled, "Panic Attack" because this is one of the things it took to get Jonathan's attention to make some serious decisions for the Lord.

Jonathan's life journey through the years has been a series of in and out of the emergency rooms and hospitals, depressed and suicidal on drugs and alcohol and trying to live out on his own and in and out of care centers and back and forth living at home, but never really going all the way with Jesus and living to please the Lord, but always living to gratify and please self in his sinful pleasures. Those of us who are living at this time in earth's history should have the testimony that Enoch had, found in Hebrews 11:5, 6, that he lived to please God.

Jonathan had moved back home to live with us, his parents on April 1, 2014. We have always tried to encourage Jonathan to give up his old lifestyle of sinful pleasures and get ready for Christ's soon return. We kept claiming Proverbs 22:6, "Train up a child in the way he should go: and when he is old, he will not depart from it." Through the years we kept praying for him, but really no real lasting change would occur, only at times our hopes would rise, only to be let down again and again, as we kept praying for Jonathan's conversion.

When we brought him home to live with us this time, he had lots of time to listen to 3ABN and speakers like Kenny Shelton from "Behold The Lamb Ministry" and Doug Batchelor from "Amazing Facts", etc. As he listened to all these sermons and pretty music on 3ABN radio and DVDs from Bill and Mary from Idaho and speakers like Hal Mayer from "Keep the Faith" and Pastor John from "Steps to Life", he began to think more serious thoughts and listen to us tell him about the Sunday Laws soon to be passed and how we need to be preparing our hearts for that time and be ready spiritually as well as physically for what's coming and to take his stand now and be true to Jesus and all His 10 Commandments and God's 7th day Bible Sabbath and not follow the beast, the papacy and his man-made Sunday sabbath. We couldn't read his thoughts, but we knew the Holy Spirit was working on his heart. We just kept praying. Then, when the Pope made his visit to the U.S.A. in September 2015, this got him really thinking more seriously. Then in October 2015 he received his official "Blessing is on the 'GO'! Evangelistic Team Member Certificate" by sending 3ABN a monthly donation. He was happy about that and hung it up in his room. I said, "God is wanting to use you as His witness! This is what we've always wanted for your life, to win souls for Jesus!

God will help you! You can do it!" Then on October 19, Jonathan had a panic attack and wanted to be taken to the Emergency room. They gave him some medicine to calm him down, but he felt himself becoming very depressed and feeling suicidal and asked the doctor to please admit him to the hospital in Topeka, Kansas for help. So, at 3:00 a.m. October 20, we drove Jonathan to the hospital in Topeka to be admitted. While there, he refused to eat anything for two days. He just stayed in bed and slept. The third day he ate a meal, brought on a tray to his room. He would read and study his Bible and pray but he wanted to just remain in his room. He continued to study and read his Bible and pray and eat only one meal a day. We encouraged him to drink water at least while he was fasting. Finally, on October 24, 2015, he was dismissed to come home.

When we went to pick him up, I looked over his discharge papers and noticed on the sheet they sent home with him was a question they had asked him, which was "What is the one thing that is most important to you?" Jonathan answered, "THE LORD". I was so proud of him and he said to me, "The Lord wants me to keep His 7th day Sabbath holy and not Sunday. And the Lord wants me to keep all 10 of His 10 Commandments. And He wants me to quit this nicotine". I said, "Praise the LORD, Jonathan! This panic attack that sent you to the Emergency room, and then on to the hospital has been like your "Damascus road" experience where you have had days of fasting and praying and studying your Bible and being alone with the LORD and listening to His Holy Spirit speak to your heart and you have responded and want to be ready for this Sunday Law coming and be true and loyal to Jesus and not go along with the Beast, the Papacy and His mark. I'm so very proud of you! I know Jesus is too! God will help you and see you through your decisions made for Him! Have faith in God and trust and rely on His promises like: Jude 24, 25, "Now unto him that is able to keep you from falling, and to present you faultless before the presence of his glory with exceeding joy, To the only wise God our Saviour, be glory and majesty, dominion and power, both now and for ever. Amen." Also, Philippians 4:13, 19, "I can do all things through Christ which strengtheneth me." Also verse 19, "But my God shall supply all your need according to his riches in glory by Christ Jesus." Also, 1 Corinthians 15:57, 58, "But thanks be to God, which giveth us the victory through our Lord Jesus Christ. Therefore, my

> *He would read and study his Bible and pray but he wanted to just remain in his room*

beloved brethren, be ye steadfast, unmoveable, always abounding in the work of the Lord, forasmuch as ye know that your labour is not in vain in the Lord."

Jonathan, this is what we've been praying for for so long! Praise God that we're getting to see and witness our son coming back to Jesus! Jonathan, I have prayed and prayed and asked God to please let you come to the Lord before I sent my book to be published, so I could write about your conversion and let the readers know you had taken your stand for Jesus and that you want to love and obey Him and not self! God bless you, Jonathan, as you continue your journey to heaven! I love you! Dad loves you! Jesus loves you! Hang in there and be strong in the Lord and let God use your life now to be a witness for Him and what he's done in your life! You've been our investment project for years and years as we've prayed God would make something beautiful of your life for God's glory! God has answered our earnest prayers for you and He has plans for your life as you stay close to Jesus and faithful to Him and His cause! Never give up. Please keep us and our son, Jonathan, in your prayers, as we'll be praying for each of you, dear reader, to make your decision to follow and obey Jesus and His counsel and love Him enough to leave these large cities as soon as possible and prepare for the crisis soon to come upon these cities and God's people, and be able to go through the storms and calamities coming and the crisis of the Sunday Law soon to come as an overwhelming surprise, as Sister White says in Volume 8 of *Testimonies for the Church*, p. 28, "Transgression has almost reached its limit. Confusion fills the world, and a great terror is soon to come upon human beings. The end is very near. We who know the truth should be preparing for what is soon to break upon the world as an overwhelming surprise." Also, in Book 2 *Selected Messages* by E. G. White on p. 142 she writes, "The work of the people of God is to prepare for the events of the future, which will soon come upon them with blinding force."

We have not time to lose! Sister White says in *Last Day Events* p. 11, "The calamities by land and sea, the unsettled state of society, the alarms of war, are portentous. They forecast approaching events of the greatest magnitude. The agencies of evil are combining their forces and consolidating. They are strengthening for the last great crisis. Great changes are soon to take place in our world, and the final movements will be rapid ones."

Sister White writes in her book, *Country Living* p. 27–28, "Let there be much praying done, and even with fasting that not one shall move in darkness, but move in the light as God is in the light… If everyone will come to Jesus in a teachable spirit, with contrition of heart, then he is in a condition of mind to be instructed and to learn of Jesus and obey His orders... We cannot have a weak faith now, we cannot be safe in a listless, indolent, slothful attitude. Every jot of ability is to be used, and sharp, calm, deep thinking is to be done. The wisdom of any human agent is not sufficient for the planning and devising in this time. Spread every plan before God with fasting, (and) with the humbling of the soul before the Lord Jesus, and commit thy ways unto the Lord. The sure promise is, He will direct thy paths. He is infinite in resources. The Holy One of Israel, who calls the host of heaven by name, and holds the stars of heaven in position, has you individually in His keeping."

May God help us all to be ready and found faithful and move under the guidance of a wise, unseen Counselor, which is God. Remember, God is in control of things. None of us know what our future holds, but we're safe as we remain in God's hands and under His tender loving care and continue to have faith in Him and His promises like Psalm 46:1, "God is our refuge and strength, a very present help in trouble." Also, Psalm 34:7, "The angel of the Lord encampeth round about them that fear him, and delivereth them." Also, read: Psalm 91; Proverbs 3:5, 6; Psalm 37:3-5; Psalm 32:8; 1 Peter 5:7.

In closing, I just want to say to my dear readers, "May this book God helped me to write be an encouragement and a help to you to do what God is calling you to do, so we all can meet at the feet of Jesus and walk on the sea of glass and the streets of gold and enjoy heaven together with our loved ones and friends where there'll be no more tears, death, nor sorrow, nor crying, and no more pain: for the former things are passed away, as Revelation 21:4 promises. This is my prayer for each of you, "Maranatha"! "The Lord is coming". God bless each of you!

"What Do People See in You?"
Written by Linda Clore, 10-9-2017

Each morning, as I begin my day, I pray that "the Lord will let me live in the sunlight of God, and radiate Jesus Christ".

Jonathan had become depressed and feeling suicidal and having a panic attack. It was around 10:30 p.m. in the evening, and he asked to be taken into the Emergency room in Ottawa for help. I got his things together and dad and I prayed with him and asked the Lord to please be with him and help him and heal him and that he would be admitted to the right place to get the help he so much needed! We hate to see him on these mental health drugs that he feels he needs, but they have all these bad side effects to put up with. But he feels he needs them, so he stays on them. We pray for his conversion and that he'll want off these bad drugs. Once he arrived at the E.R., they evaluated him and the only opening they could find to send him to for help was at our S.D.A. Hospital, Shawnee Mission Medical Center in Shawnee Mission, Kansas.

The ambulance came and they admitted him to the Mental Health floor. That was on a Thursday. We have no phone to call him or for him to call us, or for the hospital to call us and let us know how he was doing. So, all we could do was to pray for him and leave him in God's tender loving care to get well. It was 150 miles round trip to go see him, so we were asking the good Lord to please take care of him and help him get the help he needed. We were thankful he was in our S.D.A. Hospital. It was the same hospital my husband, David, worked in back when Jonathan was young and we lived in Wellsville, Kansas and raised Jonathan out in the country. Daddy worked in the Boiler and Maintenance Department at the time. It has grown into around an 800-bed hospital now.

We kept praying for Jonathan that he would get well

We kept praying for Jonathan that he would get well. Jonathan said that they would probably keep him four or five days and adjust his medicine and then dismiss him to come on home.

On Friday night, God gave me a dream. In my dream, I heard Jonathan calling, "MOM!" When I woke up, Sabbath morning, I prayed for Jonathan that he'd be doing okay. (God had given me this dream two times in the same night with Jonathan calling "MOM!")

Dad and I prayed for him and we decided to drive on up to the hospital and see for ourselves how he was doing. Since we have no phone for Jonathan or the hospital to be able to call us, we figured God was giving me a dream to encourage us to go see Jonathan and pray with him and encourage him in the Lord, and to come on home when he was dismissed and not be admitted to a depression facility.

So, dad and I prayed and made the trip up to the hospital. We had no idea when visiting hours were, so we prayed in faith that they'd let us see him. We arrived safe at 2:00 p.m., thinking visiting hours might be from 2:00 – 4:00 p.m. At the entrance desk of the hospital we found out where Jonathan was and I left a 3ABN sharing card with the lady at the desk, and she was so happy to get it. While we were there, we left cards all over the hospital and in the bathrooms. Then, we made our way up to see Jonathan on the Mental Ward.

At the patient desk, we had to sign papers who we were and when they found out we were his parents, and we had driven 75 miles up there to see our son, Jonathan, they let us go back to his room to visit with him, even though it wasn't normal visiting hours. Praise the Lord!

Before we had gone up to the hospital to see Jonathan, God had given me a poem, after I woke up that very morning on Sabbath. I wrote it out and took it up to read to Jonathan, along with another poem I had written on the day he was admitted to the hospital. The two poems were "Have Faith in God" and "More Time."

"More Time"
Written October 5, 2017

God is so merciful and kind,
He is giving us all more time.

And time to make all our wrongs right,
And laying aside all our strife.

Putting our faith and trust in God,
Preparing to walk on His sod.

To be overcomers at last,
And forgetting all our bad past.

We will trust and wait patiently,
For God to give us victory.

Through God's help we can gain power,
Receive the Latter Rain showers.

And with God's help we can press on,
And give the Loud Cry message song.

To encourage those in the LORD,
To use their Bibles as their sword.

To stand true to God and His word,
To speak with power Gods' true word.

And stand courageously for Him,
Rescuing sinners from their sins.

Then, keep our eyes on our goal,
We will be workers to win souls.

And make it to Heaven at last,
And at His feet our crowns we'll cast.

We'll thank Him for seeing us through,
And helping us His will to do.

My friends, it will be worth it all,
To be able to hear His call.

Hearing Him say, "Child, welcome Home!"
For now you will never more roam!

You're now safe in My loving arms,
For you there will be no more harm.

You've made the supreme sacrifice,
Giving up sin, with all its vice.

To have a character like God's,
Worthy to walk on Heaven's sod.

Now you can enjoy heaven's joys,
With all God's children—girls and boys.

To never more have pain or weep,
And worship at the Saviour's feet.

Enjoying the bliss of Heaven,
Singing songs of joy in Heaven.

Never more to feel sin again,
And be able to reign with Him.

Won't it be wonderful my friends,
Never to have to sin again?!

God's made this possible for us,
Just put in Him your faith and trust.

Jesus loves you, died to save you,
Now, what are you going to do?!

Friends, only you can make the choice,
To listen to God's pleading voice.

To lay your burdens at His feet,
And walk on Heaven's golden streets.

To do just that, make up your mind,
And Jesus will give you more time!

Based on: Acts 3:19

"Have Faith in God!"
Written October 7, 2017

Have faith in God,
No matter come what may.
Have faith in God,
And Jesus' will obey.

Have faith in God,
Keep your eyes on Him.
Have faith in God,
And don't let yourself sin.

Have faith in God,
To bring you through it all.
Have faith in God,
On His holy Name call.

Have faith in God,
To help you overcome.
Have faith in God,
Be ready when He comes.

Have faith in God,
Let your faith grow in God.
Have faith in God,
Then walk on Heaven's sod.

Have faith in God,
Prepare to meet thy God.
Have faith in God,
Avoid meeting the rod.

Have faith in God,
Find peace and joy in God.
Have faith in God,
By winning souls for God.

Have faith in God,
Trust Him to see you through.
Have faith in God,
And see what He will do!

Have faith in God,
And make Heaven your goal.
Have faith in God,
And trust God with your soul.

Have faith in God,
And passing every test.
Have faith in God,
Then find real happiness!

Have faith in God,
Jesus is on your side.
Have faith in God,
And in His love abide!

Based on: Acts 14:8–10; Luke 7:50; Luke 17:5; Luke 18:1–8; Luke 22:31, 32; Acts 3:16, 19; Mark 11:22–24; Amos 4:12; Hebrews 11; Galatians 3:11; Matthew 9:22, 29; Matthew 17:20, 21.

When we arrived in his room, he was just sitting in his wheelchair all alone in his private room. When he saw us, he was so happy to see us! We had prayer together and we gave him hugs and let him know how much we love him and miss him! I told him of the two dreams I had that night of him calling, "MOM!" And so we decided to make the 150 mile round trip up to see him and pray with him and encourage him to come on home, when dismissed. He just smiled and was so happy we were there! I read him my two poems that God had helped me to write and he enjoyed them.

He wanted to go out in the big room where there was a table and chairs for visiting. He got himself a cup of coffee, and I said to him, "Jonathan, coffee can cause you to be depressed." While we sat at the table visiting, I asked him to get his Bible and we'd pray and read promises from God's Word and pray and sing and have our little worship time together since it was Sabbath. Dad fell asleep in the big easy chair they had there in the room, and Jonathan and I worshipped together. As we were reading the Bible and praying and I sang some songs to him, a patient lady who looked depressed and had been walking up and down the halls came into the room where we were having our little worship, and she walked over to the phone on the wall, and then she walked over to where we were sitting at the table and she looked all around at us, and I said, "Hi", and then she just turned around and walked out. Then, within a minute, Jonathan's nurse came in and walked over to the phone on the wall, and she just stood there looking and staring at us having our little quiet worship time, and I said "Hi" to her and then after a while, without a word, she left. I thought to myself, "what are these people seeing when they come into this room and just stare at us and then without a word, they just leave?" I was wondering if maybe they're seeing a bright light about us glowing or something, as we worshipped the Lord on His holy Sabbath day? The Lord has promised in Matthew 18:19, 20 that Jesus will be in the midst of two or three gathered in His name and that if two of you shall agree as touching anything that they shall ask, it shall be done for them by the Father in heaven. Praise God!

Jonathan wanted to go to his room for a while and as we passed the nurses station, I asked if they could please call and have an S.D.A. chaplain come and have prayer with Jonathan. She was real nice and got right on the phone and said that a chaplain was on his way. I gave her a 3ABN sharing card and thanked her for her help and thanked her for taking care of my boy. She was happy to receive the card and thanked me, and I gave the other nurses, standing around behind the desk, cards too, and they thanked me and seemed interested in the information on the card.

We, then, went into Jonathan's room and I noticed his bag of clothes I sent with him wasn't there. I went out to the desk and explained that Jonathan's clothes weren't in his room. She told me that he hadn't had any clothes with him when he was admitted, and we concluded they had been either left in the emergency room in Ottawa or in the ambulance. We noticed the nurse had gotten him a couple shorts and a shirt to wear when he took his bath, and we thanked her for doing that.

While we waited for the chaplain to come and see Jonathan and pray with him, we prayed and I sang songs. The door was shut and then the chaplain knocked and came in and he wasn't an S.D.A. chaplain but was filling in for the S.D.A. chaplains who were in church that day. We let him know we were S.D.A.s and appreciated him coming and praying for Jonathan. In his visiting, he mentioned he was working on a sermon for his church Sunday morning taken from Mark 9 and that the Lord said how important it was to pray for people who are possessed. I added, it also says in verse 29 of Mark, 9, "...This kind can come forth by nothing, but by prayer and fasting." I said to him, "We've been eating light and praying for help for Jonathan to get well."

Then Jonathan spoke up and said how he had gotten into drugs growing up and took LSD, and he had a flashback that caused him to go into the hospital. The chaplain prayed for Jonathan and when he said, "Amen", then I prayed for the chaplain and his dear family he had told us about, and as I prayed for Jonathan, I had my hand on his right shoulder. When we finished praying, I gave the chaplain a 3ABN sharing card and thanked him for coming and praying with Jonathan. He seemed real interested in the card.

I then told him how when S.M.M.C. was just a little hospital before it grew to be an 800-bed hospital, how we'd bring Jonathan as a little boy to sing with us on the singing bands. And, also, when he was in his teens, he'd volunteered at the hospital as a messenger to deliver information to the different departments.

When he went to leave, I asked him if he would please leave a note for the S.D.A. chaplain to <u>please</u> come Sunday and have prayer with Jonathan. He said he would sure do that. We shook his hand goodbye and thanked him again for coming and praying for our boy. It meant so much. He said, "Let me write down your names". So, he wrote down David and Linda Clore and Jonathan.

After he left, we went back to the visitor's room and sat and prayed and read the Bible and sang. Jonathan drank more coffee.

Then, a doctor stepped into the room to visit with Jonathan and see how he was doing and adjusted his medication. He asked Jonathan what the date was and he spoke right up and said, "October 7, 2017". That pleased the doctor and I was so proud of him, too, that he could still think clear, even though he was on mental health drugs. Then, the doctor said to me, "I'm a psychiatric doctor. You know what they call us?" I said, "Yes, a shrink." He said, "That's right". After he adjusted Jonathan's medicines, he got up to leave and I shook his hand and thanked him for coming and caring for Jonathan. I handed him a 3ABN sharing card and he thanked me for it.

There was another patient that kept coming around us and wanted to talk to us and he was "way out in left field" on all the medicines they had him on, making no sense. He seemed to like us and I asked to pray for him and he said, "yes". After I prayed he thanked me and shook my hand. I gave him a hug. He thanked me.

It came time to leave and Jonathan wanted us to come back to get him on Tuesday on the 10th, so he could return home. That's when Jonathan thought they would dismiss him and for us to be there to get him. We had prayer together and we gave him hugs goodbye. I left the two poems with him to read. I thanked the nurses for letting us enjoy visiting with Jonathan and for taking care of Jonathan and thanked them for getting a chaplain to pray with Jonathan and that we really appreciated it and that he was a nice chaplain. The nurse said, "He seemed to enjoy getting to visit with you too".

We then left and headed to the Ottawa Emergency room and prayed we'd be able to find Jonathan's bag of clothes still there. Praise the Lord, they were still in the Emergency room waiting for us to pick them up! Thank you Jesus!

On the drive home, I was telling daddy all that had taken place at the hospital, since he slept through most of it.

I told him how the lady patient and then the nurse came into the room where we were having our worship and how they each just stood and stared at us and then without a word, left the room. I said, "Do you think God let them see an angel beside us or a heavenly light shining around us for them to just stare at us and say nothing?!" Daddy replied, "It seems like they had to have seen something they were staring at." He said, "You are a rare breed you know. You're friendly and outgoing and pray and witness with people and give them literature and you dress and act like a true Christian and are polite and courteous and appreciative of things you receive and people can see Jesus in you, and you're loving and kind to people and you give them hugs and you pray with people. People can tell you're a Christian and have the love of Jesus in your heart." I said, "Thank you. Praise the Lord! Thank you Jesus!"

God gave us a safe trip home, and we were so thankful God had been with us in our witnessing and so thankful we found Jonathan doing okay. Read 2 Corinthians 3, especially verse two, "Ye are our epistle written in our hearts, known and read of all men".

The date came for us to go up to S.M.M.C. and bring Jonathan home. We put more 3ABN sharing cards in our pockets and had prayer that Jonathan would be doing okay and get to come on home. We prayed the Lord would please get these 3ABN sharing cards into the right people's hands. We prayed for a safe trip up there and back again. It looked like it could storm. When we arrived, we began passing out 3ABN sharing cards. We found Jonathan sleeping in bed. We asked if he would be dismissed today and the nurses said, "The doctor hasn't made his rounds yet." Then the doctor came and dismissed him and the social worker came and wanted to make sure all was okay and Jonathan said, "yes". His nurse came in to go over his doctors changed paperwork and medicines. We gave her a card. The hospital dietitian came in to see how everything was for him to go home. She was real nice and I handed her a 3ABN sharing card and began explaining to her about the programs and how good they were and she spoke up and said, "I'm an S.D.A. too and I love 3ABN and watch it all the time!" I thanked her for the beautiful and nutritious meals they served Jonathan and how very much he enjoyed their food. She was so happy to hear that. She asked me if she could keep the 3ABN sharing card and I said, "Yes! You can order a bunch of them and share them." I said, "We've been giving them to people all over the hospital and they've all been very happy to get them!" She said, "That's good!"

When she left, a lady with her Dalmatian dog was standing outside Jonathan's door. Jonathan said to her, "Please bring your dog in here." The lady came in with her dog and we petted the dog and she said, "I bring my dog here once a month for the patients to see her do tricks". She began having her dog do all kinds of tricks. I asked if she was a teacher? She said, "Yes". She said, "People are taught and trained and dogs have to be taught and trained too. Obedience is so important to learn." I thought to myself, "Yes, obedience to God and His word and His will is so important for people to learn too, so we can rightly represent Jesus and His truth and prove what we believe and live it, so we can be a blessing and a help to others and make Jesus happy and proud of us. Just like that lady was so proud of her dog showing others what she had learned from her master and making her master happy and the people watching the dog were made happy. Jesus wants us to be like Him in word and deeds, so we can bring joy into other people's lives too and be good representatives and good witnesses for Jesus by the things they've learned and live. Read 2 Timothy 2:15.

We then were directed off the floor for Jonathan to return home. We thanked everyone for Jonathan's good care he had received.

When we got into the car, we prayed for a safe trip home. On the way home, it just poured and poured and poured and it was so very hard to see and cars and trucks were just flying around us so fast in the rain, but praise the Lord, we arrived safely home! Thank you Jesus! And we were so thankful to have our son safely back home with us and doing okay. Praise the LORD!

As we all three were visiting at home and going over the rain storm God had just pulled us through and how it poured so hard, and we couldn't see and we kept praying and praying for God's watch care over us and to protect us, even though our wipers would not go real fast to clear the rain off our windshield! They were on slow speed and we could not get them to go fast, so we couldn't see the road. We felt God had spared us from having an accident and saved our lives! Praise the Lord! Thank you Jesus! We know the devil would love to snuff us all out and get rid of us for witnessing all over the hospital and me writing another book to encourage people to remain true to God in the storms ahead of us and the Sunday crisis, and we'll have to have faith and trust for the Lord to take care of us through those trying and dangerous days ahead of us who will remain true and faithful to Jesus and His 7th day Bible Sabbath and all His 10 Commandments. We felt God had overruled Satan, who was keeping our wipers on slow speed, so we couldn't see the road, and we were driving by faith, trusting the Lord to send angels all around us so we didn't have a bad accident and be killed! David went out and checked the wipers, and they have a fast speed and a real fast speed, but the old devil was keeping them from working, so we couldn't see the road in the bad down pour. David saw that they are working just fine now!

We also talked about how Satan would love to have Jonathan put out of the way, so he wouldn't be converted and win souls for Jesus either. Satan tries to keep Jonathan on these terrible devil drugs with all their dangerous side effects, even making him depressed and suicidal. God keeps pulling Jonathan through these terrible experiences he's been going through on Satan's drugs, and God keeps overruling Satan and sparing his life, so he can work for Jesus and win souls from Satan to the Lord's side. We just keep praying for God's help and protection to see all three of us through Satan's attacks he brings on us to destroy us! Praise God, our God is stronger than Satan! We were also remarking to one another about the things that were happening while we were waiting for Jonathan's doctor to dismiss him. I was going over how the head nurse kept opening Jonathan's door to tell us things and then she'd shut the door and leave.

One time she left the door opened up all the way so she could look from her desk right in at us. We had been praying and I was singing songs and read out of Jonathan's Bible promises and we were handing out 3ABN sharing cards with all who came into Jonathan's room. I remarked to David and Jonathan as we went over the experiences we had with the nurse who kept opening Jonathan's door to say something to us, then she'd close it, then she finally left it open so she could look in and see us. I said to David and Jonathan, "I wonder what she was seeing in there when she kept opening the door and would say a little something and then close the door, then she finally left it all the way open and left. Do you think she was seeing a heavenly glow like maybe the other head nurse on Sabbath, when we were there seeing Jonathan and having a worship time with him, and she came in and stared at us, like she was seeing something, like a heavenly glow about us?" We all remarked that we may never know, but things were happening that was surely strange and we couldn't account for it.

It makes you wonder what people see in you when they look at you and observe your life?

Sister White says in *Patriarchs and Prophets* on p. 144, "From every Christian home a holy light should shine forth… they would indeed be the 'light of the world'". Matthew 5:16 says, "Let your light so shine before men, that they may see your good works, and glorify your Father which is in heaven."

In *The Great Controversy* book by E. G. White, we read on p. 612, "Servants of God, with their faces lighted up and shining with holy consecration will hasten from place to place to proclaim the message from heaven. By thousands of voices all over the earth, the warning will be given."

Like the song I had in one of my dreams called "Breathe on me Breath of God."

1. Breathe on me, Breath of God,
   Fill me with life anew,
   That I may love what Thou dost love,
   And do what Thou wouldst do.

2. Breathe on me, Breath of God,
   Until my heart is pure,
   Until with Thee I will one will,
   To do and to endure.

3. Breathe on me, Breath of God,
   Till I am wholly Thine,
   Until this earthly part of me
   Glows with Thy fire divine.

4. Breathe on me, Breath of God,
   So shall I never die,
   But live with Thee the perfect life
   Of Thine eternity.

"It is His purpose that every Christian shall be surrounded with a spiritual atmosphere of light and peace. There is no limit to the usefulness of the one who putting self aside, makes room for this working of the Holy Spirit from his heart and lives a life wholly consecrated to God". Read also *Ministry of Healing* by E. G. White, p.58, especially this quote: "Amidst the hurrying throng, and the strain of life's intense activities, he who is thus refreshed will be surrounded with an atmosphere of light and peace." Read also *Patriarchs and Prophets* by E. G. White, p. 329 about the light that illuminated Moses' and Stephen's face in their experiences

Read *Review & Herald* July 4, 1899 and *Acts of the Apostles* by E. G. White p. 153

Read *Faith and Works* by E. G. White p. 65 and *Review & Herald* June 30, 1896

"The Seizure!"
Written by Linda Clore on October 22, 2017

Jonathan has been having pain in his right shoulder and low back. Many months ago the doctor ordered an x-ray of his right shoulder and they came to the conclusion it must be arthritis causing all the pain, and why it was hard for him to move it. Off and on he'd take pain pills for it, but he'd become addicted to the pain pills and had to be taken off the pain pills.

This pain in his right shoulder and in his low back was making him very uncomfortable, so again he asked for some pain pills to give him relief for a while from his pains.

The doctor ordered a one week supply until he had it x-rayed again and possibly he'd have to have surgery on his right shoulder.

The day he was to go get his x-ray and have the doctor surgeon examine him, he had a seizure in his chair. He had taken more pain pills than he should and most of his medicines he's on cause seizures as a side effect.

Dad and I were sitting at the breakfast table and from where I sit at the table, I can look into the front room and see Jonathan sitting in his chair. I saw him shaking all over and his arms moving furiously. I ran into the front room to him and knew immediately he was having a seizure! Dad and I both were frantically praying God would please help him and spare his life. He was chewing on his tongue and blood was coming out of his mouth onto his beard. His eyes rolled back in his head, and he stopped shaking and fell over to one side. Dad was crying and saying, "He's dead! Check his pulse!" His pulse was slow and real faint. I kept calling his name, "Jonathan! Jonathan!" He wouldn't respond! His eyes began to stare and were glassy looking! His face was blood red! I put cold washcloths to his face and neck. Dad said, "That's how red my mom got just before she died!" and I said, "Yes, my dad's eyes glazed and stared and glassy looking just before he died, just like Jonathan's eyes are looking right now". He was sweating and I took off his shirt and turned the fan on him. We kept praying and trying to arouse him and help him and call his name and tell him, "You're okay Jonathan! You're going to be okay! Jesus is helping you!"

He slowly started to come around. I asked him who I was? He didn't know. I asked him the date. He didn't know. I asked him how he felt? He said, "My stomach hurts." I asked his name; he didn't know. I said, "Jonathan, let's take you to the Emergency room and let them check you over." He got out of his chair and started to crawl toward the door, then he got back into his chair. I said, "Jonathan, you need medical help! Please crawl for the door and get in your wheelchair, so we can get you into the car and take you to the Emergency room". He again got out of the chair and started rolling back and forth, from side to side on the floor. Then got back into his chair saying, "I don't want to go to the Emergency room".

We kept praying with him and explained to him that he had had a seizure. He began to know his name, who I was and where he was, but still didn't want to go to the Emergency room. It took a while for him to get awakened to what had just happened to him. He said he still couldn't remember things, but it was slowly coming back.

We prayed and thanked God he was still alive and doing okay. We had just witnessed a miracle!

Several days later he said, "I need to make another appointment to see the doctor and get an order for an x-ray on my right shoulder that hurts".

I said to him, "You said you didn't want to go through a surgery on your shoulder".

He said, "But I'd like to have an x-ray and see why I'm in such pain." I said, "the last x-ray showed you have arthritis".

I said, "No more pain pills."

He said his right eye was hurting real bad and he needed to have the doctor look into his eye and see why he's in such pain, ever since he had the seizure.

He went to the Emergency room in Ottawa and the doctor had a CT scan done on his head, and Praise the Lord, everything checked out okay! Thank you Jesus! Jonathan said his memory was back to normal too! Praise the Lord!

I said, "God has certainly been looking out for you!" We all agreed and prayed and thanked the good Lord for healing Jonathan and seeing him through this terrible experience".

Jonathan said it was such a horrifying experience he went through!! It was for us too! But God saw us through it all! Praise God!! Thank you Jesus!

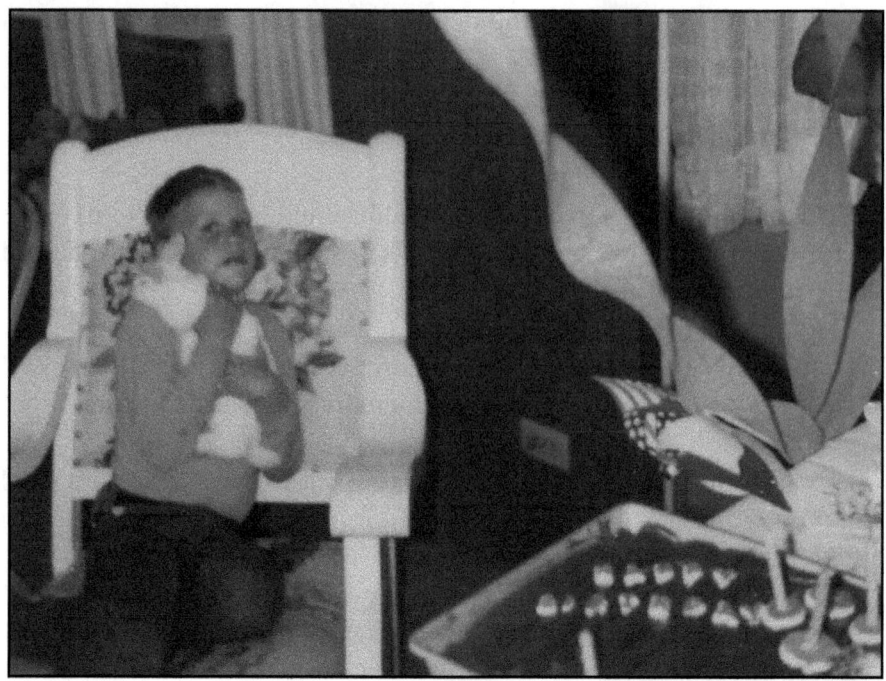

Jonathan, age 6, April 21, 1976, with pet rabbit, "Bunny Girl."

Jonathan, age 8, with church school teachers in Oklahoma.

Jonathan with Linda, living in the country.

Jonathan, age 8, at his baptism.

Jonathan with Elder W.D. Frazee, his mother, and Linda at Kansas Camp Meeting.

Jonathan with David in the Wellsville, KS home.

Jonathan with David, learning to garden.

Jonathan, age 13, in front of our little cabin in Tennessee.

Jonathan, age 22, ready for work at McDonald's.

Jonathan, age 22, riding his bicycle.

Jonathan's Journey | 83

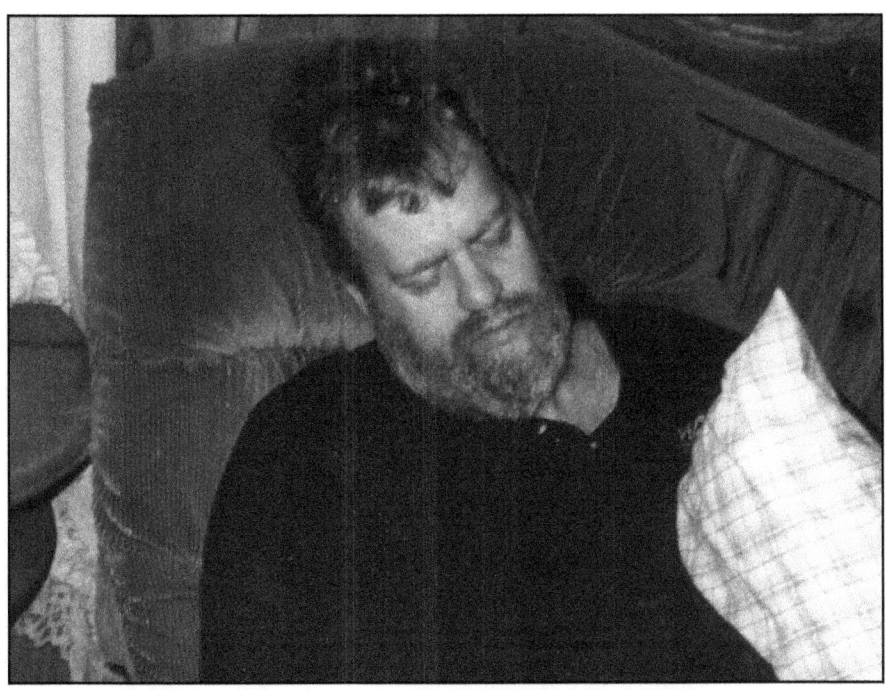

Jonathan, age 47, sleeping in his recliner in the front room.

2007 Dodge van that God helped us get.

David Clore digging in our garden with one of the cabins in the background.

The Lincoln Mark VIII, given to us by Cindy and Lisa.

On the "Ark," our 14-acre sanctuary.

Our front yard with buildings on the "Ark."

Linda Clore, age 74, taken in Summer, 2017, on the "Ark."

STAY TUNED FOR THE NEXT EPISODE OF "JONATHAN'S JOURNEY."

(Like the song says, "Never Give Up! Jesus is Coming!")

AB ASPECT Books

We invite you to view the complete
selection of titles we publish at:
www.ASPECTBooks.com

We encourage you to write us
with your thoughts about this,
or any other book we publish at:
info@ASPECTBooks.com

ASPECT Books' titles may be purchased in
bulk quantities for educational, fund-raising,
business, or promotional use.
bulksales@ASPECTBooks.com

Finally, if you are interested in seeing
your own book in print, please contact us at:
publishing@ASPECTBooks.com

We are happy to review your manuscript at no charge.

www.ingramcontent.com/pod-product-compliance
Lightning Source LLC
Chambersburg PA
CBHW070545170426
43200CB00011B/2561